THE MULTINATIONAL COMPANY

ORVILLE L. FREEMAN

PRAEGER

PRAEGER SPECIAL STUDIES • PRAEGER SCIENTIFIC

Library of Congress Cataloging in Publication Data

Freeman, Orville L.
The multinational company.

Includes index.
1. International business enterprises.
2. Underdeveloped areas—International business enterprises. I. Title.
HD2755.5.F737 338.8'8 81-717
ISBN 0-03-059052-3 AACR2

Published in 1981 by Praeger Publishers
CBS Educational and Professional Publishing
A Division of CBS, Inc.
521 Fifth Avenue, New York, New York 10175 U.S.A.

123456789 145 987654321

Printed in the United States of America

Acknowledgments

Many people contributed far beyond the call of duty in "accomplishing" this volume. First came the task of getting together the materials on which the many presentations I have made over the years rested. My colleagues at Business International (BI) all contributed to that process. I am deeply obligated to them, especially my dedicated and competent assistant Beverley Varoli. The laborious process of refining the volume of materials down to book size began with Truman Becker, once a BI correspondent in Australia, currently with the Asian Development Bank. The process was completed by Ralph Diaz, editor of *Business International*, who carefully and methodically reviewed the various articles and presentations concentrated by Becker and skillfully tied them together to make the final product. Through the entire process Ruth Karen, director of BI Public Policy Group, played a very prominent and vital role. In most of the articles and presentations her gifted pen and wise insights played a major part in marshaling ideas and information in an effective manner. So to Beverley, Ralph, Ruth, and Truman, this expression of affection, respect, and appreciation.

Contents

Introduction

The multinational company (MNC) is one of the least understood and most important institutions in the world today. It has been praised and vilified; all forms of powers have been attributed to it, so much so that it often appears to be bigger than life. Numerous questions continue to be asked about this relatively new phenomenon on the world scene:

—For what purpose and whose benefit does the multinational company exist?
—Are the benefits a country secures greater than the costs it bears by admitting an MNC?
—To whom is the MNC really accountable?
—What effect does the MNC have over the sovereignty of a nation and a government's ability to effect policies important to the development of its economy?
—Should the MNC's decision making and operations be controlled? And if so, how?
—What does the development of the MNC mean for future global economics?
—Indeed, what is the future of the multinational enterprise form itself?

There are no easy answers to these and other questions relating to the MNC, but the key to understanding the issue lies in the definition and scope of such enterprises. A multinational company is one that looks at the world as one market, which it services by combining resources, manpower, technology, capital, and other production factors from various places, at sites where this combination can be done efficiently and profitably. Of course, many things get in the way of this goal: pressures for local equity and management control by host countries, labor and government pressures in the home country, and the difficulty any manager faces in becoming free from thinking narrowly and less than globally.

Regardless of such constraints, the MNC appears to be moving toward, and indeed requires, a one-world economy free of barriers to movement of goods, people, and capital. In a sense, it is closer to achieving the linkages required for a coordinated approach to world economic and social problems than are any of the global political institutions, such as the United Nations, created since World War II.

However, the MNC is not without its critics. It has been condemned for its supposed global reach. A charge hurled against the MNC is that it usurps political power and undermines the legitimate aspirations of individual countries. It has been accused of seeking to keep part of the world in a state of easy exploitation and of playing cold-blooded games with jobs and economies of developed countries, for the sake of profits and power.

The purpose of *The Multinational Company: Instrument for World Growth* is to correct this image and to remind all concerned—critics, corporate executives, government officials, and the public at large—of what MNCs can do to alleviate the problems facing the world in the 1980s. Some of the book is aimed at executives, prodding them to think in terms of the bigger picture. Some of it is intended to persuade officials to bear in mind that the powers of the MNC should be harnessed but not cut off. All of the book will give the general reader an understanding of the MNC that is essential.

The 12 chapters of the book are based on speeches and articles presented by Orville L. Freeman, president and chief executive officer of Business International Corporation. Mr. Freeman is in a good position to comment on both sides of the issue. He was secretary of agriculture under Presidents John Kennedy and Lyndon Johnson, a role that placed him at the working center of international discussions dealing with the world's critical food problem. In his ten years with Business International, a research, consulting, and publishing company covering world business conditions and practices, he has met with numerous political leaders and consulted with the heads and other key decision-making executives of virtually every multinational company.

What he has to say has not always been pleasing to MNC executives or popular with government officials. He strikes a middle position or "third way" in the conflict between nation-states and MNCs that is enlightening, provocative, and informative. Mr. Freeman feels that the MNC is an enormous force for good. Its achievements, however, will depend on the extent to which executives can broaden their horizons and adapt to needs, and the degree to which government officials are willing to understand the vital role MNCs can play and to refrain from interference.

Until recently most multinational companies were United States-based. Now, European-based companies are becoming important, as a result of their increased size, need to broaden their markets, and stronger currencies that allow them to buy foreign assets fairly cheaply. They are shifting attention from national to global production and are beginning to see the world as a potential market. If present trends continue, multinationalization is likely to increase greatly in the 1980s as giants from both sides of the Atlantic, from Japan, and from the newly industrialized countries (South Korea, Taiwan, Brazil, and Mexico) strive to penetrate each other's markets and to establish bases in less-developed countries, where there are few indigenous concentrations of capital sufficiently large to operate on a world scale. This rivalry may be intense at first, but will probably abate through time as firms approach some kind of equilibrium. A new structure of international division of labor will be born.

So profound a change in economic structure will require correspondingly radical changes in the legal, political, and ideological frameworks. At present, "practice is ahead of theory and policy," says Mr. Freeman. "Multinational corporations, through their everyday business practice, are creating a new world environment, but policy makers are lagging behind." In other words, the situation is a dynamic one. Right now we seem to be in the midst of a major revolution in international relationships as modern science establishes the technological basis for a major advance in the conquest of the material world and the beginnings of truly cosmopolitan production.

Multinational companies are nearly in the vanguard of this revolution, because of their great financial and administrative strength and their close contact with the new technology. Governments are far behind, because of their narrower horizons and perspectives, as are labor organizations and most nonbusiness institutions and associations. Therefore, in the first round, multinational corporations are likely to have a certain degree of success in organizing markets, making decisions, and spreading information in their own interest. However, their success will create tensions and conflicts that will lead to reactions by other groups.

Thus, whether direct foreign investment can continue to grow at 10 percent per year, as it has since 1960, considering the drastic implications such an expansion has for world order, is an open question. Although economic factors, in the sense of an expanding world market, are favorable, political factors are a different matter; and economic power cannot long be out of phase with political power.

The Multinational Company: Instrument for World Growth endeavors to accomplish the following objectives:

—Present many of the key characteristics of the MNC.

—Describe the circumstances leading to its emergence and growth.

—Highlight the role of MNCs in developing countries.

—Illustrate how the march of the world toward global interdependence has not been matched by the growth of international institutions.

—Discuss some of the major environmental factors that influence and are influenced by the MNC.

—Explore the likely paths of evolution of this new phenomenon.

The Multinational Company: Instrument for World Growth does not pretend to offer ready-made answers to these and other complex problems. It does, however, provide the student and the researcher, as well as the government or business executive, with a wealth of information from which a better understanding of the current and emerging characteristics may be gained.

"The MNC: An Overview" is an introduction to the role of the multinational company in today's world. In this chapter Mr. Freeman explores basic attributes and achievements of the MNC as well as some of its shortcomings in the past, stressing ". . . the fact is that times have changed. Exploitation under modern-day conditions is minimal and a danger far outweighed by the potential benefits. . . ."

In "The MNC: Whose Interests Does It Serve?" Mr. Freeman takes another look at MNCs, the milieu in which they operate, and why they are such a strong force for the building of global institutions and—more effectively than present halting political efforts—for global economic cooperation. In essence, MNCs are already doing globally what the United Nations and other organizations were meant to accomplish. The stress is on the uniqueness of the MNC and why it should be encouraged and not circumscribed.

"How MNCs Must View the World" is a plea to MNC executives to recognize the forces that are shaping the global environment and to learn to accommodate them. Mr. Freeman identifies five global "motivators" that must be understood by companies, as well as some overriding geopolitical issues. The fundamental question is ". . . whether the world will continue to move toward universalism, erasing the boundaries between countries and encouraging trade, investment, and competition, or whether it will revert to nationalism and mercantilism."

In "The Corporate Public Policy Imperative" Mr. Freeman discusses the need for managers to pay the same attention to public policy matters that they do to ordinary aspects of doing business. This theme is followed up in "Communication: Key to Corporate Survival," a key chapter that states who are the MNCs' stakeholders, and who are their critics—and why there is opposition and what can be done about it. In Mr. Freeman's summary, "the problem is that business is not accustomed to explaining itself in terms of values. It is experienced and adroit in marketing goods and services. It is neither experienced nor adroit in selling the values that animate it and that it contributes to society."

In "Questionable Corporate Payments Abroad," Mr. Freeman contradicts currently popular mythology about international business practices, particularly the question of bribery. He states that these do not constitute the essence of the way companies do, or want to do, business but, rather, that such payments are a matter of extortion, not bribery; they are demanded, not offered. As one executive put it to him, "If business is based on payoffs, you can finally go out of your mind, because you lose control. It's just no way to run a railroad."

"Risk and the Future" deals with the political and economic risks of operating abroad, and what can be done to minimize any inherent threats to the peaceful environment that MNCs require to thrive.

Mr. Freeman's views in "Prospects for Government-MNC Relations" are somewhat controversial, but on the mark concerning the viability of the relationship between the public and private sectors. He points out that in a free-market economy such relations have to be adversarial, in the sense of checks and balances similar to those in the U.S. government between the executive and legislative branches. Such a relationship is needed in order for government and business to remain responsive to a free society. It is only to the degree that a government steps beyond certain limits that the system is endangered.

"The Antidote for Worldwide Stagflation: A Global Marshall Plan" takes a look at what went wrong in the 1970s and what can be done in the 1980s. This is a key chapter, in which Mr. Freeman summarizes a position he has maintained since the early 1970s—that a three-way cooperative effort involving MNCs, OPEC capital, and developing countries must be undertaken to broaden the world's market base and productive capacities. The same basic theme is seen in "The MNC and the Fourth World," in which Mr. Freeman states that MNCs have a crucial role to play in bringing the Fourth World countries into the economic mainstream. He goes on to examine a possible solution: a "broker" who would bring together MNCs and local governments for worthy projects.

"The LDCs: Victims and Victors of Commodity Price Increases" again deals with developing countries, which Mr. Freeman maintains are critical to the solution of world economic problems. In this chapter he takes a not very popular stance by advocating more commodity agreements and giving the reasons why such arrangements, worked out on an equitable basis, are necessary.

Finally, "The MNC and Latin America: Friends or Foes?" makes an important point by virtually saying "a plague on both your houses" unless governments and MNCs learn to consider each other's worth and values. The chapter ends with a good checklist of "do's" and "don'ts" for MNCs to follow.

The appendix to this book summarizes an ongoing study by Business International on the critical question of whether outgoing investment cuts jobs at home and on the question of what values and contributions incoming foreign investment transfers to the host country.

In conclusion, *The Multinational Company: Instrument for World Growth* is designed for both the student and the practitioner. The 12 chapters provide insights into the operations of the MNC and into the world in which it operates. The book also contains an excellent group of readings on international companies and their relationship with the Third World.

1
The MNC: An Overview

The chapter below is adapted from a paper submitted by Mr. Freeman for the First Global Conference of the World Future Society, held at Toronto in July 1980. It is a good introduction to the role multinational companies can play in the world today. Starting with a definition of a multinational company, the author goes on to explore accomplishments and shortcomings of this remarkable type of enterprise. Four key attributes of MNCs are presented to show what these companies could do for future world development. In summary the author demonstrates that foreign direct investment by MNCs is a win-win proposition for both home and host governments.

Foreign direct investment by multinational companies (MNCs) could be a very important factor in furthering desperately needed economic development in most countries of the world. Unfortunately, today there is no unanimity of support for such investment. Instead, a great many people and organizations around the world are hostile to MNCs, charging that, rather than making a contribution to the well-being of both host and home countries, foreign investment exploits the receiving country and "exports" jobs from the home country.

There are many definitions of an MNC. An MNC is a company that produces and markets goods and services in more than one country, looks at the entire world as its area of operations, and acts accordingly. It searches everywhere for new technology, talented people, new processes, raw materials, ideas, and capital. It thinks of the entire world as its market, and strives to serve customers everywhere. It produces goods wherever they can be produced economically or renders services to one or more markets at a profit, regardless of national boundaries or ideologies.

Multinational companies today play a vital role on the world economic scene. Direct investment by MNCs has reached a level of over $350 billion, $164 billion of which, according to the U.S. Department of Commerce, is by U.S. companies. These companies turn out about one-third of the world's gross product, in the neighborhood of $1.25 trillion worth of goods and services. Since 1960 the growth of these companies has averaged in excess of 10 percent per year, double the rate of economic advance in the industrial countries during the same period.

Since about 1977, according to some estimates, the expansion and growth of MNCs has decelerated. It is true that the overwhelming presence of the U.S. MNCs, which have made about 60 percent of the foreign direct investment in the world, has diminished somewhat since 1975, with a downturn in the level of capital flow from the United States. The new factor in this world picture is the flow of foreign direct investment into the United States in record quantities, rising at the rate of 14.5 percent a year in the 1970s, compared with 6.7 percent in the 1960s and 7.4 percent in the 1950s. So, although the U.S. MNCs continue to expand, measured against world expansion the U.S. dominance has been eroded somewhat. Nonetheless, a U.S. decline in relative size is not an absolute decline in position. Most major U.S. corporations depend on their overseas operations for an astonishingly large proportion of their sales and, in most instances, an even larger proportion of their profits.

Such dramatic growth and expansion figures highlight the fact the MNCs have played a key role in the remarkable economic growth the world has enjoyed since World War II. In effect, a new kind of comparative advantage has emerged. In addition to the historic definition, penned by David Ricardo, that stipulates that countries trade with each other whatever each can produce most efficiently, today we find MNCs locating their centers of activity wherever they can bring together the most efficient combination of technology, capital, and people to produce and market most profitably.

Much of the technology, management talent, and private capital needed to solve the world's economic problems is controlled by MNCs. Further, they have the capacity to move resources, capital, and management skills as a package of productive factors, custom tailored to the requirements of a given project. This differs from the deployment of experts and technicians for technical assistance, although those programs have an important role and value of their own. It is the package effect of moving resources in combination that makes multinational companies so highly competitive. It also gives them a special capacity to transfer know-how to others in a learn-by-doing, on-the-job situation, which is most effective.

Since the end of World War II the world has moved a long way from protectionism toward universalism and toward an open world for trade and investment. Multinational companies have been on the cutting edge of that development. Taking advantage of rapidly improving communications and transportation, MNCs have been a powerful force in hurdling national boundaries and restrictions, so that trade, commerce, goods, services, and ideas can flow more freely, to the benefit of all mankind.

There are four reasons why these strongly affirmative statements emphasizing the importance and potential of foreign direct investment by MNCs can be made. First, the multinational corporation is a powerful force for peace. In its own interests it seeks to minimize disruption and conflict between nation-states, and to further a uniformity of tax, patent, and copyright laws, trade practices, and all the rules of the economic game worldwide, so it can reach out under common rules to serve the mass market. In the global shopping center, which the world is increasingly becoming, antagonism between nations, jingoism, and restrictions on the flow of money, goods, people, or ideas are all anathema to the MNC. At the same time, its process of reaching around the world, searching always for the most effective production constellation, brings the nations and the peoples of the world closer together, identifies the international problems that must be solved, develops a global social conscience, and experiments upon and tests the practicality of different organizational techniques to meet international problems.

Second, the internationalization of production and services carried out by MNCs is a powerful element in generating the levels of economic growth necessary to global progress.

Third, most of the technology that is desperately needed in the developing world if growth is to take place has been developed, and is owned and controlled by the private sector. It is proprietary, has been created at great cost, and is considered a very valuable property by the companies that own it. In 1980, the U.S. Supreme Court recognized even the patentability of living organisms, a decision that will encourage further private-sector research in genetic engineering. The result should be improved products and health-delivery services, not just in the Unites States and in the developed world, but in the developing world as well. International pharmaceutical firms will be among the major developers of these new products and systems, and they will move these products and systems wherever they are needed.

Fourth, international companies have a special capacity to deliver technology. This goes beyond what is commonly called high technology, to include management capacity and marketing know-how. The distinctive aspect of the role that MNCs can play most effectively (far more so than governments) is not so much the transfer of resources as such, but the impact of moving those resources—whether they be capital, technology, or management skills—as a finely honed combination of productive factors, tailored to the needs of a given opportunity or project. This is not yet recognized by most governments. For example, Mexico, anxious to encourage growth of an indigenous pharmaceutical industry, is forcing Mexicanization of foreign-owned firms in this sector. The industry position is that its contribution in pure research and technology, which appears in improved products, is matched by its ability to test, market, deliver, and train—in short, to manage.

The complementary capacity for efficient utilization that comes when a complete package of productive factors is geared to the competitive needs of a given opportunity or project is crucial. The backstopping service of head office staffs and laboratories, with access to procurement channels and marketing outlets, and the ability to mobilize and deploy around the world are also important characteristics of the package that makes possible the unique contribution by the MNCs. In short, the MNCs enable Third and Fourth World nationals to learn by doing in the crucible of the competitive marketplace.

We have only to look at South Korea, Mexico, and India for examples of this learning by doing. Each of these countries is producing budding multinationals of its own. Indian companies are beginning to apply their considerable technical and managerial skills in Africa, the Middle East, and Southeast Asia. Korean contractors and suppliers are among the most aggressive entrants into the fast-growing Middle East market. Mexican giants like Visa and Alfa look to the United States and other markets to supplement their growth at home. Were it not for the impetus and example of international companies from the United States, Europe, and Japan that are active in these three markets, these developing-country enterprises would not be looking beyond their own borders.

So far, however, the extent of MNC investment in and transfer of technology to the Fourth World countries is minimal. A recent study by the United Nations points out that MNCs are primarily investors (at a level in excess of $300 billion) in industrial countries. The estimated $68 billion invested in developing countries is concentrated in the so-called middle-income developing countries: Brazil, Mexico, Venezuela, Nigeria, Malaysia, Indonesia, and a few others. Only 15 percent has gone to economies with a per capita income of less than $200 a year, which is where the major problems lie.

If, then, MNCs have the technology needed and the capacity to deliver it in a form that will maximize its effectiveness in building the economy and well-being of the receiving country, and are not now doing so, it would seem that organizations that want to regulate MNCs should give careful attention to how the necessary involvement by MNCs in Fourth World countries can be accomplished.

There is great confusion, emotion, and not a little demagoguery on the subject of foreign direct investment and multinational companies. Some of the political leadership of the Fourth World countries—and not a few academics in the developed world—condemn and attack MNCs as exploiters. In country after country, conditions, regulations, and requirements are being put in place that are difficult to meet and that sharply diminish the attractiveness of the country in question for investment purposes.

Despite a track record that in the main is a positive one, MNCs are highly controversial. They are constantly under attack by populists because they are large and powerful. No international body exists with authority to enforce standards of conduct, and this accentuates the criticism that MNCs are uncontrolled. The fact that they are subject to the laws, regulations, rules, and practices of every country where they do business—which in the case of large MNCs means doing business all over the world—resulting in a maze of often conflicting and overlapping requirements, is ignored by populist critics.

Multinational companies also have become the whipping boys of contending political factions. Witness India today. The U.N. General Assembly and the Transnational Commission of its Economic and Social Council provide forums for frequent demagogic attacks. Agribusiness MNCs, which invested significant time and effort in the Industry Cooperative Programme of the Food and Agriculture Organization, have been driven out and attacked by forces opposed to private enterprise for trying to infiltrate the United Nations. In many countries commitments made to private investors by government leaders have been breached for political reasons or through ineptness and failure to follow through.

The net result is that many MNCs are "turned off." They are increasingly selective. And an entire new profession has cropped up: country risk-assessment, which helps companies in the selection process. There are many places where companies can invest. There is great competition for technology. Why, MNC executives understandably ask, should they take the risks and encounter the lack of appreciation and cooperation that so often faces them when they make investments in the Fourth World?

This is not to suggest that international companies are paragons of virtue and selflessness. They have been guilty of abuses, and of what can be described as exploitation, in some developing countries. Rape of the environment has taken place. Abuse of the consumer has occurred. On occasion monopoly has resulted. Such abuses, combined with the vivid recollection of the colonial period and gunboat diplomacy, have left a residue of bitterness and antagonism.

As a result valid, searching questions are being asked throughout the developing world. Will the multinational corporate package benefit the host country in the long run? Is there a danger of overspecialization? Will the business in question become merely a branch plant of a larger operation without any real expansion of its economic base, thereby failing to move toward what is considered a necessary diversification in the host economy? Will the spillover of the MNC enterprise stimulate new production, or will it only create tensions as a handful of new, highly paid jobs attract people to the urban area, exciting expectations that cannot be fulfilled? These are legitimate questions. They call for thoughtful, thoroughly prepared, well-documented, and well-publicized answers.

But the fact is that times have changed. Exploitation under modern-day conditions is minimal and a danger far outweighed by the potential benefits that would flow from major investment by

MNCs in Fourth World countries. In the main, MNCs today are performing at a high level of service and integrity. If they do otherwise, they will be severely penalized. Today the smallest country is more powerful within its borders than the largest company. It is increasingly able to detect abuses and shortfalls and to retaliate appropriately. So are the international media. In short, exploitation does not pay.

There is no doubt that foreign direct investment is a win-win proposition for both the host and the home countries. This conclusion is based not only on the qualitative evaluation advanced thus far in this paper; it is verified quantitatively by thorough research conducted by Business International since the early 1970s.

As might be expected, the massive increase in the activity of international corporations did not go unnoticed. And, as expected, the main noticers were critics of business. By the mid-1960s two separate sets of critics of the international corporation had come into existence. One group's frame of reference was the host country, the country to which the foreign-based corporation brings capital, technology, knowledge, and management, and where it establishes local manufacturing and marketing operations. This group's criticisms centered on how the foreign corporation exploited the host country, how it unfairly competed and monopolized, how it limited the political freedom of the host country—often recently gained.

The other group's reference point was the country from which the foreign investment was made, the capital-exporting country. This group's criticisms centered on the export of jobs as companies moved production facilities to foreign, low-cost production centers and imported products back into the capital-exporting country. It focused on the loss of capital investment in the capital-exporting country, and on the balance-of-payments weaknesses resulting from the outflow of capital. The main expounders of the job-export theory were the labor unions.

In the late 1960s in the United States, the Burke-Hartke Bill, which emerged from this viewpoint, was proposed. The bill called for the imposition of controls on capital outflows by corporations; for punitive taxation of foreign corporate investment; and for quotas on imports into the United States. The proposal was so extreme that it evoked a strong negative reaction among those who advocated free international trade and less government interference in economic decisions.

Business International (BI) decided to examine the job-export theory closely. Was it true that foreign investment by U.S. corporations "exported" jobs? Was it true that foreign investment by U.S. corporations reduced capital investment in the United States? Was it true that foreign investment by U.S. corporations weakened the dollar?

An initial check was made with ten U.S.-based companies that had invested a great deal outside the country during the 1960s. They were asked how many employees they had in the United States at the beginning and end of the 1960s. Common sense suggested that if the job-export theory were valid, American companies that had been investing a great deal outside the United States would be employing fewer people in the country. What BI discovered was that these ten companies had not decreased their job roles in the United States during the 1960s. Indeed, they had increased them a good deal faster than the average U.S. manufacturer.

This quick survey, however, was not rigorous enough to do more than cause some doubt about the validity of the job-export theory. Indeed, it could be criticized on several grounds. For example, labor union critics suggested that U.S. companies that invested overseas increased their U.S. job rolls, despite the exporting of jobs, by acquiring other companies in the United States. Other critics contended that these firms could have increased employment in the United States even faster during the 1960s if they had not invested abroad.

BI therefore embarked on a far more exhaustive research program, the findings of which resulted in our publication *The Effects of U.S. Corporate Foreign Investment, 1960-70*. In this study BI requested detailed information on a wide range of sales, export, import, capital investment, and financial flow factors, as well as on employment figures in and outside of the United States. Questionnaires were sent to more than 500 companies, and BI received 125 usable responses.

The findings were amazing. Every conceivable test of the job-export theory was tried—and all failed. Indeed, the facts indicated that corporate foreign investment was associated with a faster increase in U.S. employment, rather than the reverse.

The findings were so unexpected that BI was asked by the chairman of the House Ways and Means Committee to repeat the study for the period 1960-72 to see if the results would be the same. They were. We have continued to update the research each year since then, in order to keep testing it and to see if the results changed as world conditions changed during the 1970s.

As of 1980, eight studies have been completed for various time periods. Each has a different sample because different companies responded each time, although a number of companies have responded in all or most cases. One of the studies was carried out specifically in response to the criticism that U.S. companies that did export jobs did not respond to the questionnaire, and therefore the findings of the studies were invalid. To correct for that possible bias, we limited the next study to the 100 largest U.S. manufacturing companies listed in *Fortune*, covering the period 1960-75. The findings confirmed those of the other studies.

BI's major findings are described in the appendix to this book. They cover the issues of employment, exports, imports, trade balance, balance of payments, investment in the United States, and investment in host countries.

The conclusions BI verified were supported in dramatic fashion, so far as benefits to the host country are concerned, in a lecture delivered by the prime minister of Singapore, Lee Kuan Yew, at the World Conference of the International Chamber of Commerce, Orlando, Florida, on October 5, 1978.

In that lecture the prime minister gave full credit to international corporations for the Singapore "miracle" whereby, as he put it, the 2 million people who faced disaster in 1965 had advanced to a level of economic well-being that is the envy of the developing world. He gave credit for "mopping up unemployment running at 10 percent of the work force in 1960" to U.S., European, and Japanese MNCs.

"It could never have been achieved," he emphasized, "at the pace at which Chinese and Indian Singaporean enterprise was slowly moving in 1960 from traditional retail and entrepôt trade into new manufacturing or service industries." Comparing MNCs with Singaporean entrepreneurs in the 1960s, he pointed out that only 6 percent of wholly owned U.S., European, and Japanese enterprises failed, while the wholly owned Singaporean enterprise failure rate was 38 percent. He went on to point out that when Singaporeans went into joint ventures with U.S., European, or Japanese companies that provided the know-how, experience, and marketing, the casualty rate went down to 7 percent.

Lee Kuan Yew summarized Singapore's experiences as follows:

> My experience leads me to conclude that developing countries get their industries going with good indigenous managers, provided they have experienced foreign co-managers to show them what

> not to do in the early stages. Singapore's development would not have been possible of it had not been able to plug into the world grid of industrial powerhouses in America, Europe, and Japan.

On the basis of his experience, the prime minister advised that other developing countries should be encouraged and helped to plug into this grid. How soon and how effectively they can tap in, he said, depends on them, and on how realistic and pragmatic their governments are in their politics, so as to strike a bargain with those who have the capital, technology, and management know-how to help produce goods for their own people and perhaps also for export in the competitive international markets.

> In other words, the more rationally governments take advantage of their relative backwardness and low wage costs, the more benefits they will derive from the international division of labor. For them not to try is to court more misery, more coups, more totalitarian and, eventually, more communist regimes.

So far in this presentation and analysis of international companies in the world economy, the approach has been a broad, macroeconomic one, as it has sought to evaluate both qualitatively and quantitatively the position of MNCs in the world's economy and the effect of these companies on world peace, increased productivity, and the internationalization of production by moving technology, particularly to the developing world. I would now like to focus specific attention on the Fourth World, countries with a per capita income of less than $200 per year, where privation, malnutrition, and human misery multiply. How can the technology, the learning process described by Prime Minister Lee Kuan Yew, be moved into these Fourth World countries where human need is so great and, as a consequence of its being unmet, the threat to the stability of civilization grows to explosive proportions?

First, it must be recognized that there exists a real problem of communication between MNCs and the leaders of developing countries regarding investment decision-making. In 1978, BI held a roundtable at Geneva with the United Nations and its specialized agencies. It was an excellent roundtable, but poorly attended by MNC executives, who are "turned off" by the United Nations and by the developing world, for reasons noted above. However, even the sympathetic executives who participated, and the top officials in the U.N. agencies who served as discussion leaders, were talking at, rather than to, each other for most of this interchange. The U.N. officials did not understand that international companies in the private sector make investments based upon an assessment of risk and return, and that they are influenced only marginally by the fact that the Fourth World countries constitute a great human need and moral challenge, and present a threat to the peace and stability of the world.

Fourth World political leaders seem unable to grasp the elementary fact that private companies are not charity institutions, and must be responsive to standards set in the competitive, worldwide business environment as reflected in the performance demands of boards of directors, shareholders, and the securities markets. To be sure, some lip service is paid on occasion to the general statement that, of course, an investment by the private sector must be reasonably profitable; but the lip service is just that. It is not translated into comprehension, let alone action.

Unfortunately, most of the time developing-country leadership tends to voice harsh demands, more often than not based on the contention, implied or expressed, that to make a profit is somehow an immoral endeavor. On the other side of the table, there is a lack of awareness and sensitivity on the part of business executives to the political problems of the government leaders in the Fourth World countries. Business leaders are sometimes arbitrary and tend to shrug their shoulders, saying, "If it is this complicated and difficult, and if we are received with such suspicion and reservation, we will invest elsewhere."

We at Business International think it imperative to review carefully ways to improve communication and to achieve better understanding of the respective points of view where foreign direct investment is concerned: the standards that a chief executive officer of a multinational economy is held to by the board of directors, the shareholders, and even the employees, and the political hazards to which a Fourth World political leader is subjected by his constituency when he appears to be closely identified with MNCs.

Decision-making executives of MNCs have judgmental limits within which they can take the risk of investing in a Fourth World country if they feel that the political leadership is reliable and that they can depend on commitments made. If there is a reasonable assurance that an appropriate return will be forthcoming, even though, in some cases, the time span for the return must be extended and the risk is greater than it would be if the company invested elsewhere, many chief executive officers will go ahead. This is especially true in cases of developing countries with long-term potential, where a strong executive can carry along the board and shareholders by convincing them to take additional risks in return for the long-term future gains.

There is a role for an independent organization—perhaps in the United Nations, perhaps not—that can review and make recommendations of how potentially profitable opportunities can be called to the attention of possible MNC investors, and how a possible investor can be brought to the attention of the relevant Fourth World country. An effective "honest broker" could perform an important function in bridging the gap between country leadership and company decision makers.

Such a broker would have to be a person of experience and substance, held in high enough regard to have access to the top decision makers in both developing countries and multinational companies. Such a person could alert the respective parties to a potential mutual opportunity and, if his credibility were of high enough order, get both sides seriously interested. Once that was accomplished, the company and the country would have to communicate with each other and, one hopes, negotiate a mutually beneficial arrangement. However, the starting point would be the evaluation, by a highly credible individual or team, that an opportunity exists that might meet the investment standards of both company and country.

Unfortunately, foreign direct investments that meet minimum standards of return are not numerous in the Fourth World countries where the need is the greatest. For the most part, in these countries, the necessity for private sector-government cooperation has not yet been recognized. I contend that it must be—and the sooner the better—if the needs of the Fourth World, needs that are both desperate and dangerous, are to be met.

2

The MNC: Whose Interests Does It Serve?

The following chapter continues the probing look at multinational corporations from the point of view of the global institution building that is necessary for world peace and economic development. The author considers this one of the key functions of these companies that must be kept in mind when asking whose interests it serves. A striking analogy is made between the situation facing international companies today in the world and the problems created in the United States at the turn of the century, when a growing number of local companies started to expand to national status. This chapter is based on a speech the author gave at the Foreign Policy Association conference held in New York on April 9, 1973.

To get at the question "Whose interests are served by the multinational corporation?" a definition is in order. A multinational corporation is an international business institution, typically a large one, that makes direct investments outside its country of origin. It usually engages heavily in trade, but in addition it manufactures in one or more countries outside its home base.

Multinational corporations serve the interests of the people who work for them. They are major employers who since 1960 have increased employment and wages, both in the United States and around the world, substantially faster than noninternational companies.

Multinational corporations serve their shareholders. As a general rule they have expanded their capital and increased their production about twice as fast as purely national companies.

Multinational corporations and those they serve cannot be understood or evaluated without identifying and measuring the place of international companies in the world of today. Measuring U.S. multinational corporations on the scale of their effect on the United States alone is dwarfed by the importance of their place on the world scene and what it means to the future well-being of mankind.

Certain fundamentals must be kept in mind when examining the role of the multinational corporation:

—The post-World War II world has been shrunk to the size of a grape by the modern technology of transportation and communication. This shrunken world faces momentous and critical common problems—problems that defy nation-state solutions. Pollution and the ecology, the population explosion, limited natural resources, the energy gap, and the growing disparity between the wealthy one-third and the poverty-stricken two-thirds of the world—these are only some of the threats to mankind's future. Unfortunately, none of these threats can be met by nation-states acting singly. All require worldwide, cooperative problem-solving and resource/technology mobilization.

—Progress toward international political institutions capable of moving effectively to the solution of these worldwide problems has been painfully slow, almost nil. I do not denigrate in any way the United Nations or its affiliate agencies when I say that, so far, its actions in the world have been dominated by the politics of the nation-state; it has not moved out to build the international institutions needed to solve urgent international problems.

—While institution building on the international political front has been minute, on the private economic front it has been extraordinary. Since World War II great strides have been taken toward what might be called the internationalization of production. The world has moved swiftly toward a unified economy.

An analogy can be drawn between this process and what happened in the United States after World War I. Manufacturing then was concentrated on the eastern seaboard, and companies exported to the rest of the country, which reacted with a high degree of sectionalism and parochialism. I can well remember my father, a small merchant, violently resentful of the factories and stores that came to Minneapolis, Minnesota, financed by eastern capital. "Those so-and-so's on Wall Street," he would say, "come here to exploit our community. They send the profits back to New York. They make all the decisions in the board rooms on Wall Street." The sectionalism of my father, and thousands like him, had little effect. The U.S. Constitution prohibited state and local restrictions on the flow of goods and capital.

I remember well the Minnesota of those days: largely agrarian, with some important mining activity, commerce on a limited scale, but not very much manufacturing and very little manufacturing on a national scale—let alone an international scale.

Today, when I go home to Minnesota, I visit companies like 3-M and General Mills, Multifoods and Medtronic, Cargill and Control Data. I don't have to tell you that these are not only major national companies; they are also important international firms. And the prosperity of the state, and the living standards of its people, have risen immeasurably in just about every way.

The resulting mass market reaching from coast to coast has been the single most important reason why the United States has the highest standard of living in the world. It triggered large industries that utilize modern technology and develop modern management techniques.

Now the same process, reaching toward a unified global economy, is taking place around the world. Its instrument is the multinational corporation, which can aptly be called an economic workhorse for the world. The process is a slow and tortuous one, for instead of having one central bank, one currency, and no tariffs, as was the case in the United States, the internationalization of production is taking place in a world with over 100 central banks, over 100 different currencies, and countless tariffs and other restrictions to trade and the free flow of investment. Nonetheless, in recent years the world has moved toward a unified economy with breakneck speed.

Multinational companies, not only American but also European and increasingly Japanese, are reaching all over the world, seeking the most efficient combinations of technology, people, and resources to produce and distribute at the lowest possible cost to the consumer and with the highest profit to the shareholders. More and more companies are developing a global social conscience as their shares spread around the world and top management begins to reflect the nationalities of the countries where they do business.

Until recently this process of internationalization of production commanded little attention. Trade, rather than investment, has historically been the object of concern, professional attention, and media presentation. However, now, the place of international production, the multinational corporation, and the significance of the movement toward unifying the world's economy has come strongly to the center of attention. The nation-state, with its "religion," as Arnold Toynbee calls it, of national sovereignty, has reacted strongly to the apparent threat from the multinational corporation, whose ownership and final control is located outside the political boundaries of the nation in question. There is a very real danger that out of this confrontation could come a serious retrogression to the nation-state dominance of yesterday, which would halt the movement toward an economically unified world.

By now the thrust of my analysis is, I am sure, clear:

—The multinational corporation, economic workhorse of the world, makes it possible that a decent standard of living can be attained by a world population that will reach 6 billion-plus by the year 2000. No other institution has the skills and innovative strength needed to master the technology and the organizational and managerial skills that—together with cash flow and borrowing power—are necessary to raise the world's production to the level needed to meet the demands of an exploding population and to reverse the widening gap between a world that is one-third prosperous and two-thirds poverty-stricken.

—The multinational corporation, with its capacity to move resources of capital, technology, and management skills as a package of productive factors tailored to the needs of a given opportunity or project, makes an indispensable contribution to many less-developed countries (LDCs). Such a "package of productive factors" is to be distinguished from the deployment of experts or technicians as a part of technical assistance programs. Such a package, plus the backstopping of multinational head office staffs and laboratories, and access to procurement channels and marketing outlets around the world, provides unique and necessary services to LDCs desperately seeking to improve the standard of living of their people.

—The multinational corporation is today the single most powerful force to put the world together and make it possible to develop the international institutions essential to solve the world's pressing problems. Further, and for the same reasons, the multinational corporation is a powerful force for peace in the world. In its own interests, it seeks to minimize disruption and conflict between nation-states and to further a uniformity of taxes, patent and copyright laws, trade practices, and all the rules of the economic game worldwide, so it can reach out under common rules to serve the mass market, the global shopping center that the world is increasingly becoming. Antagonism between nations, superpatriotism, restrictions on the flow of money or goods or people or ideas are all anathema to the multinational company. At the same time, its process of reaching around the world, searching always for the most effective production configuration, brings the nations and the peoples of the world more closely together, identifies the international problems that must be solved, develops a global social conscience, and experiments with and tests the practicality of different organizational techniques to meet international problems.

No one can predict with any assurance how the current confrontation between the process of internationalization of production and the religion of national sovereignty will end. At the moment the nation-state seems to be moving into ascendancy in more developed and less developed countries alike. Nonetheless, in many guises and in many places, the multinational corporation continues to grow. One hopes that the people in the world seeking economic betterment will grudgingly yield national sovereignty and the world will gradually develop the international institutions necessary to take advantage of the great potential for meeting mankind's needs that has come on the scene with science and technology. Should that happen, and as an optimist I say it must, the greatest force in accomplishing that purpose will be found not on the political front but, rather, on the economic front. The primary instrument in carrying forward that process will be the multinational corporation.

3
How MNCs Must View the World

The chapter below is extracted from Mr. Freeman's address at the Emhart Corporation's International Management Conference, held in June 1980 at Pompano Beach, Florida. The aim of the author here is to get executives responsible for international operations to understand the forces that affect the working environment in which MNCs must function and to learn how to live effectively with them. He feels that the MNC's global perspective is an important factor on which it must trade when dealing with governments and critics. The chapter outlines five "motivators" shaping the world, as well as key geopolitical and geoeconomic issues.

Today thousands of companies consider the entire world as their area of operation, and act accordingly. They search everywhere for new technology and processes, talented people, raw materials, ideas, and capital. The entire world is their market, and they strive to accommodate customers everywhere by manufacturing the goods and rendering the services that can be produced economically.

This process—the internationalization of production—is the other side of the coin of comparative advantage, a trade phenomenon that David Ricardo and John Stuart Mill documented so effectively in the nineteenth century. Ricardo pointed out that it is to the advantage of all when nations produce what they can most efficiently turn out, and exchange those products with other nations that can produce other needed items more efficiently.

Today multinational companies (MNCs) around the world bring together raw materials, finance, research, technology, distribution, communications, and marketing—all of the factors essential to high levels of productivity and efficiency—in optimal locations where the best results, in terms of serving the market and making a fair return, can be obtained. This new kind of comparative advantage makes a vital, important contribution to building a better future for all. This is true not only in terms of producing goods and services and making a profit, but also of leading the movement toward a world that is integrated economically as well as politically.

Narrow nationalism that leads to concomitant mercantilism and protectionism is the primary threat to the future well-being of mankind. The great British historian Arnold Toynbee dramatically identified this threat in an article he wrote in the 1960s, "The Reluctant Death of Sovereignty." In it he described this unhealthy type of nationalism as a cult that has become mankind's major religion, a religion whose God is a Moloch to whom parents are willing to make a human sacrifice of their children, themselves, and all of humanity, too, if conventional war should escalate into a nuclear one.

GLOBAL PERSPECTIVE ESSENTIAL

One of the tasks of international business is to respond to the threat of narrow nationalism by teaching people to understand that the global approach that guides MNCs is the most viable way for the world to reach the levels of production needed to make basic goods and services available to people everywhere. It is the only way to eliminate hunger, poverty, and despair. By doing this the world can be moved to a more centralized structure, in which $450 billion a year is not wasted on preparing armaments and nuclear weapons for a war that will end not only all wars but all civilization.

There is no doubt that, as a world, we have the resources, technology, research capacity, management know-how, and capital to sustain growth. The question is whether we can get these together efficiently and fast enough for the necessary adjustments, and build international institutions responsive to the reality of global interdependence. Can we avoid being overwhelmed by the resurgence of narrow, jingoistic nationalism and protectionism that threatens from countries on all sides?

This is the major challenge that lies before us in the 1980s: whether the world will continue to move toward universalism, erasing the boundaries between countries and encouraging trade, investment, and competition, or whether the world will revert to nationalism and mercantilism, raising walls between countries and limiting competition. Or, to pose this critical question in another way, has the liberal, internationalist dream of the post-World War II era ended? Are we in the process of reverting to autarkic nationalism and mercantilism? Or will the realities of interdependence among countries and peoples, which has grown almost exponentially since the mid-1950s, continue? In plain words, which will prevail in the historic confrontation of the 1980s—nationalism or universalism?

FIVE GLOBAL 'MOTIVATORS'

In order to develop strategies and tactics for doing business in the world today, we must first understand the standards, values, and philosophies that shape the motivations of mankind. Such values today are common to mankind virtually everywhere as a result of the advances in modern transportation and communication. Five such motivators stand out: humanitarianism, egalitarianism, rising expectations, participation, and nationalism.

Humanitarianism is a powerful motivator. All over the world people know and care that others are suffering, whether it be through famine, earthquake, or unemployment. Until recently people often didn't know what was happening beyond the borders of their neighborhood, and if they knew, they cared little. Today they know that in this modern age of science, technology, and engineering and managerial know-how, poverty and deprivation are not necessary; they are the result of technical or managerial shortfalls, and they can and should be corrected. This universal caring is a powerful force in a world in which as many as a billion persons remain in hunger, poverty, and deprivation.

There is also a great spirit of egalitarianism around the world. It demands equality of opportunity, of course, but it also demands more. It seeks, in some fashion, the equivalent of the good things of life that everyone wants to enjoy: food, clothing, housing, transportation, recreation, beauty, art, and culture. This drive for egalitarianism is linked to rising expectations. People know what others have, and as a result seek more, and often demand more. Here we find the basic explanation for the shifting emphasis in the Western world from increased productivity to improved living standards and the elimination of poverty. This "motivator" is one of the basic reasons for worldwide, double-digit inflation.

Another basic motivator that has come strongly to the fore is participation. Everywhere people want a piece of the action, whether it is in the company—seeking better working conditions, or a larger part in decision making, or more prestige, or more consideration and respect from superiors—or to be heard and permitted to shape policies and programs in their own countries. I have just visited South Korea. I was in Brazil not long ago. These advanced developing countries in different parts of the world are examples of two highly centralized, fundamentally totalitarian governments that are now feeling their way as they seek to respond to popular demand. They are trying to develop workable institutions that are more democratic in nature, permitting wider participation without breaking down essential order and stability.

These same motives are the driving force that shapes the demands for a new international economic order made by the Group of 77, which includes over 125 countries, as developing nations. These are the driving forces that MNCs must understand. Every manager must respond to these while operating within the governmental framework of the country in which the firm or plant is located. These, in effect, put a new face on nationalism, the fifth of the motivating forces.

We tend to think about nationalism in company terms as the threat of expropriation or a forced division of a contract or other arrangement. Indeed, that has been the case in the past. However, dramatic instances of expropriation, as in Chile and Cuba, and now in Iran, are relatively few and are not likely to take place frequently in the future. They are usually the product of major ideological changes. Today the thrust of nationalism is one of the continuing encroachments on MNCs' freedom to operate. It involves regulations, taxation, restrictions, price and wage controls that are increasingly directed toward foreign companies. This means that MNCs operating in host countries must be sensitive and professional in their relations with governments that increasingly have the will and the sophistication, as well as the power, to press demands on MNCs.

A NEW DIMENSION OF MANAGEMENT

I submit that this new face of nationalism calls for an entirely new dimension of management, particularly when the interest of an MNC operating on a world scale may deviate from the development plan of the host country. Such a case calls for tact, sensitivity, and understanding. Areas of common interest between company and country must be emphasized, and those areas in which interests may diverge must be attended to. Obviously this is easier said than done. The process calls for basic comprehension of the values, philsophies, aspirations, culture, and expectations of the people in the countries where business is done.

My first major point, then, in evaluating the forces that must be understood is that people's motivations, their values, what they think, what they perceive, and what they demand must be adequately factored into a company's strategic plans and operating decisions in every country and every community in which the MNC does business. The new dimension to this truism of "people importance" is the universality of the motivational forces that drive people today.

A second major guidepost on the world scene that is of great importance to corporate planning and operations, outside of the threat of nuclear war, is inflation: double-digit, global inflation. It is a cancer eating the vitals of the world economic system. It has replaced depression and mass unemployment as the number-one economic and political issue. The moral values of honesty, industry, and saving, which are the underpinnings of a productive, growing society, have been gravely eroded as confidence in the future diminishes, making such values seem to represent an irrational course of action.

Why save for a rainy day when savings won't buy an umbrella? Why be scrupulously honest and work hard when there is no long term on the horizon? Instead, people begin to reason more and more that it makes sense to make as much as you can, as fast as you can, with the least effort and in almost any way possible. Hence, the old concept of a fair day's work for a fair day's pay goes out the window, as far as the worker is concerned.

INFLATION FALLOUT

Inflation takes its toll in other ways. We see a cautious approach to capital investment on the part of the businessman. For the investor it means channeling funds away from productive investment and into inflation hedges. For society as a whole, it means saving less and spending more, with predictably negative consequences for long-term economic growth.

All this makes for uneasiness and a lack of confidence in basic economic institutions and their future viability. Society's basic institutions are questioned today because of inflation, just as they were questioned in the 1930s because of deflation and 30 percent unemployment. Apprehension is such that a major economic event or failure of a prestigious financial institution could trigger lagging confidence into panic and, with it, accelerate the recession into flat-out depression such as the world suffered in the 1930s.

It is well to keep in mind that the inflation that began in the 1970s and that has carried over into the 1980s is not the creation of the OPEC oil monopoly. Rather, it can be traced back to the basic values referred to earlier—mainly humanitarianism and egalitarianism—reflected in the overall demands that hardship and suffering be rectified quickly, regardless of the cost, and the insistence that the world's wealth be more evenly and fairly divided, regardless of the effect on production. In other words, dividing the wealth rather than producing it has become a priority. We shouldn't forget that in 1973, before the advent of OPEC, every country in the world, including the United States, suffered from high inflation. Then OPEC struck.

Hardly anyone had forecast that the oil-rich countries—particularly those in the Middle East, with their deep antagonism toward each other—could come together to form the most massive, most successful cartel in history. Their action and the continuing acceleration of the price of oil—and, with it, of energy, which climbed 150 percent in 1980—has made it extraordinarily difficult to control the accelerating inflation cycle. Higher costs of other natural resources have also contributed to inflationary pressures. In effect, in the heady days of the 1950s and 1960s, the world pumped the oil closest to the surface, cut the most reachable trees, and mined the most accessible minerals. This is not to say that the world is running out of natural resources, as the Club of Rome contended a few years back. Rather, the fact that these resources are more difficult to reach, and require more technology and money to obtain, contributes to inflation. All of these pressures continue to make it extremely hard for governments to conquer inflation by applying traditional fiscal monetary policies.

Particularly critical and dangerous at this time in history is the irresponsibility of the OPEC countries in continuing to raise the price of oil. There is little indication that in the future they will help to bring global inflation under control. Instead, they insist on increasing their real income from oil by increasing prices, reaching toward a somewhat nebulous standard that they call the marginal cost of alternative energy sources. As nearly as can be determined in reviewing that term with OPEC leaders, it means the cost of synthetic fuel, such as gasoline from coal, presently a $50-per-barrel equivalent to oil and projected to rise to a $100-per-barrel equivalent by 1990.

Inflation has penetrated deeply into the world economy. Nevertheless, a few countries, mainly West Germany and Japan, have had the determination and toughness to make sacrifices; they appear to have it under control. The citizens of both of these countries are, of course, more disciplined by history than those in the rest of the free world. Their governments have wisely followed tough monetary and incomes policies by limiting wage increases to productivity gains.

This could be done in Germany because of a deep-seated anti-inflation psychology, the consequence of the frightful post-World War I inflation suffered by the German people. In Japan the homogeneous, orderly society built from the ashes of World War II has always kept productivity, rather than equality, as its primary goal. Following such a policy, Japan survived both the early inflationary explosion that took place at the turn of the 1970s and the impact of OPEC oil prices, despite the fact that it must import 90 percent of its energy.

Whether the world—for it will take a global effort—will coordinate and cooperate to contain and control inflation is the key to the future. It won't be easy and it won't be done in a rapidly expanding economy. The world will contain inflation by decreasing consumption, increasing productivity, and imposing discipline in order to sustain an incomes policy. In my judgment it will take at least until 1985 to force the current 9-10 percent inflation level down to a livable 2-5 percent.

So for the next few years, as business leaders look to the future, the realization that growth will be more limited than would be possible if inflation were under control must be faced as a basic fact of life. This requires careful planning, high productivity, excellent motivation of the work force, and sensitive community relations, all adding up to exceptional management. The marketplace in which they do business will be tough and competitive. Profits can and will be made, but only the best-prepared will get a staisfactory return.

PRESSURES FROM THE GROUP OF 77

Another major global phenomenon—one that has a potentially serious impact but that also holds promise for the future—lies in the developing world, which is currently designated as the South, as compared with the North, or industrial world.

The economic growth and improvement in human well-being enjoyed by the North has not, for the most part, been shared by the South. Most people in the North enjoy a standard of living infinitely superior to that at the turn of the century. More people in the South suffer poverty, privation, malnutrition, and, in many areas, starvation than ever before. In a world dominated by humanitarianism and egalitarianism, where modern communications dramatize this great discrepancy, such a circumstance is dangerous and threatening.

As a result the demands of the South, the so-called Group of 77, have accelerated. With increasing shrillness they have denounced the industrial world as colonial exploiters whose progress and wealth have been gained at the expense of millions of deprived people around the world. They insist that a massive shift of world resources to rectify the exploitation and to improve the well-being of suffering people must take place. The term being used for this shift is "new international economic order," known by its acronym, NIEO. This NIEO is demanded with all due haste and without strings.

In the main the NIEO demand has fallen on deaf ears. Identifying the limits of management experience and political instability in the developing countries, the North has replied, "Why should the common people of the North, struggling to improve their own well-being, sacrifice to make possible aid to the South that seldom reaches the needs of the hungry many and only makes the rich richer?"

So the North and the South continue to talk—and sometimes shout—past, rather than to, each other. The magnitude of the problem and its threat for the future are set forth accurately and dramatically in the report of the Brandt Commission, and also in the report of the Presidential Commission on World Hunger, on which I was privileged to serve. Abraham Lincoln once said, "A nation cannot exist half free and half slave." World leaders are increasingly saying today, "The world cannot progress half well-off and half in poverty."

Let me moderate what is basically a very bleak and, I think, dangerous world situation by pointing out that very striking progress in improving the well-being of their people has been made in some of these countries. This group is made up of a dozen or so of the more than 100 developing countries that are called ADCs (advanced developing countries) or NICs (newly industrialized countries). In Asia they include South Korea, Taiwan, Singapore, Hong Kong, and perhaps Malaysia. Mexico and Brazil are examples in Latin America, as are Portugal, Spain, and Greece in southern Europe. And, of course, there is the subcontinent of India.

Let us take one example, South Korea. Despite current political turbulence and a sharp economic downturn in 1980, a literal miracle has taken place in that country. Per capita income has climbed from $75 a year in 1957 to over $1,600 in 1978. Increasingly the ADCs have incorporated modern technology and have, for the most part, built increasing food production into their economic structure. They have sustained a real economic growth rate of 5-15 percent yearly, even during the mid-1970s recession. Some economists contend that if the developing world generally had not maintained its rate of economic growth and continued as an important demand factor on the world economic scene, with increasing imports from the North, the serious recession of the 1970s would have collapsed into deep depression. This may or may not be true, but there is no doubt that the developing countries have become a very powerful factor in the overall world economy.

MUTUALITY OF INTERESTS

For example, 25 percent of the manufactured exports from the United States go to the nonoil-producing developing world. If food products and the OPEC countries are added, the figure climbs toward 50 percent. The developing countries are as great a market for U.S. exports as all of western and eastern Europe and Japan combined.

Unfortunately, this excellent record of economic progress by a handful of ADCs does not mean that the great masses of the people in the South have enjoyed any significant improvement in their well-being. On the contrary. The Presidential Commission on World Hunger concluded that some 400 million—and probably closer to 800 million—people in the developing world suffer grave nutritional deficiencies. This tremendous human need can be met only by a world whose economy is expanding. Major investment of capital and technology must be extended to these countries so their economies can grow rapidly enough to extend benefits to the masses. Here again, OPEC and oil enter the picture.

Few of the developing countries are blessed with oil. Countries with tremendous economic potential, such as Brazil, face a heavy adverse balance of payments because of their massive oil imports. Today there is an enormous accumulation of debt in the developing countries and of dollars in the OPEC nations. When OPEC first raised prices in 1974, it was widely predicted that the world's monetary system would collapse. It seemed impossible at that time to recycle the enormous shift of wealth, by far the greatest in history, that had moved from the industrial world to the oil-rich OPEC countries.

The world monetary system proved far more responsive than anyone had predicted. The OPEC wealth was effectively recycled. The primary institution accomplishing this extraordinary feat was the private banking system, but an enormous increase in the level of global debt owed by developing countries to private banks has resulted. The potential for recycling a second enormous shift of wealth to the OPEC countries is almost impossible in a world in which economic growth seriously lags.

I predict that we will hear increasing reference to a global Marshall Plan (see Chapter 9) as world leaders strive to develop politically acceptable and economically feasible formulas. A totally new relationship is evolving among the industrial world, the developing countries (particularly the NICs), and OPEC. The success of such a three-way partnership is a key to measuring the future. International companies' management should keep this in mind in their strategic planning. Whether the world will regain the growth rate necessary to resume the advances made during the 1950s and 1960s will depend in large measure on whether the mutuality of interests of North and South can be effected.

GEOPOLITICAL ISSUES

It is always tempting to sidestep the geopolitical issues, for they seem almost beyond measured analysis. Businessmen tend to focus on global economic forces. However, critical developments on the world political scene demand consideration. Their likely consequences must be considered as part of companies' strategic planning.

In 1980 the leaders of the major industrial nations struggled through another session of summitry, this time in Venice. Although the results were more decisive and clear-cut than at earlier summit meetings, it is not at all certain that what was agreed upon will be carried out. To be sure, summitry is important. It represents, at least potentially, a major step forward; but implementation of what is agreed upon is still subject to the political forces in the nation-states, whose policies and directions are shaped and moved by local interests, including the deep emotional commitment to country rather than to world.

There are, of course, many difficult, sensitive, and complicated geopolitical forces in the world. Each of them has heavy overtones of emotionalism. They reach back in history, triggering almost uncontrollable emotions, acts, and events. Witness the Israeli-Palestinian confrontation; the Basques in Spain; the never-ending problem of independence for Northern Ireland; the demands in Quebec; the bitter drama in South Africa; the recent revolution and near anarchy in Iran.

Obviously, all of these ongoing emotional geopolitical forces affect the world's stability. How, then, can MNCs do business, and how can the world advance to the goals of human betterment? Given time, patience, and firmness, all of these explosive situations can be contained and significantly moderated. However, there is one overriding geopolitical issue that dominates the world and must enter into any analysis of the future. I refer, of course, to the enigma that is the Soviet Union.

What does the USSR have in mind? Where does it plan to move? How can it be contained? During the 1970s the world lived with a very uneasy détente between the United States and the USSR. The confrontation of the immediate post-World War II period was modified somewhat, even as confrontation followed confrontation—from Berlin to Korea to Vietnam, and now to Afghanistan. Soviet hegemony over eastern Europe was regretfully accepted by the Western world. The invasion of Afghanistan, however, is another matter. It has clearly shaken to the very core, if not exploded, the détente of the 1970s.

Many people in the West, acknowledging Soviet paranoia about that country's security (remember how frequently it has been invaded), were prepared to accept the growing Soviet military power, including nuclear weapons, until it reached equivalence with that of the United States and the Western world. Those who followed this line of thinking hoped that once the Soviets did reach this parity, their enormous investment in military power would taper off and the balance of power would be maintained.

Unfortunately, this has not been the case. It appears that military equivalence has been reached, but rather than tapering off, the Soviet Union continues to increase its enormous concentration on military hardware and nuclear devices. Soviet aggression outside its accepted orbit has taken place with the Afghan invasion. The détente of the past appears to have lapsed into no détente, as the West and the USSR move into a harsh confrontation.

The key question is what the Soviets are up to. No one can answer that question; not even now, with the current aged leadership, and certainly not in the future, when new, younger, presumably more aggressive leadership takes the helm. The risk from overwhelming Soviet armaments and nuclear superiority is too great. The threat to human freedom and the open market economy that the West treasures so highly is real.

There is little reason to doubt that the USSR will continue its expansionist policy as long as it thinks it can get away with it, and that the commitment to Marxism as a world ideology and the major universal historic force continues. The hundreds of billions of dollars of capital poured into armaments could provide an enormous stimulus to the world's economy if channeled into peaceful pursuits.

The best we can look for in the immediate future is a very uneasy power confrontation. Perhaps when the Soviets recognize the resolution of the West and its determination to check Russian hegemony, and when they are forced by their own citizens, as their economy falters under heavy diversion of resources to the military, they will seek accommodation. This is the hope for the future. In the meantime there appears no choice but to counter Soviet military power, regardless of the cost to the economies of the free world.

4
The Corporate Public Policy Imperative

This short chapter, which is extracted from Mr. Freeman's remarks at a seminar on the business environment at George Washington University in July 1979, has one simple theme: international executives must pay the same attention to public policy matters that they usually devote to other parts of doing business, such as financing, engineering, and marketing.

Since the end of World War II, the world has moved a long way from protectionism toward an open world for trade and investment. Multinational companies (MNCs) have been on the cutting edge of that development. Taking advantage of rapidly improving communications and transportation, MNCs have been a powerful force in minimizing national boundaries and restrictions, so that trade, commerce, goods, services, and ideas can flow more freely, for the benefit of all people.

This is not to say that all MNCs are an unmitigated boon. Abuses of power and failure to live up to high standards of integrity and performance have taken place. Like other powerful institutions, MNCs could benefit from better checks and balances. Such checks and balances are provided primarily by stockholders, consumers, and national governments. But I also think more light on murky areas would be beneficial. As Justice Louis Brandeis once said, "Sunlight is the best disinfectant." However, in the main, I am convinced that MNCs today are performing at a high level of service and integrity. The fact is that if they do otherwise, they will not be able to survive. Today the smallest country is more powerful within its borders than the largest company. It is increasingly able to detect abuses and shortfalls, and to take appropriate action.

On balance, MNCs have contributed significantly to the world's progress and, if given the opportunity, will continue to do so. However, despite a record that is mainly a positive one, MNCs are highly controversial. They are constantly under attack by populists simply because they are large and powerful. That there is no international body with authority to enforce standards of conduct accentuates the criticism that MNCs are uncontrolled. Populist critics conveniently ignore the fact that MNCs are subject to the laws, regulations, rules, and practices of every country where they do business, which in the case of large MNCs means doing business all over the world, coping with an enormous maze of often conflicting and overlapping requirements.

Socialists, who advocate government collectivism and do not believe in the market economy, private enterprise, and the profit system, are constantly chipping away at MNCs, which they make a special target. Another group of supercritics of MNCs is the extreme nationalists, who in the host country resent ownership of a productive asset by any foreigner, and who in the home country charge—with equal passion, especially in the United States—that when MNCs invest abroad, jobs are exported and the home economy suffers. Early in the 1970s the attack on U.S. companies investing abroad reached a high level of intensity and vitriol, leading to the Burke-Hartke Bill, which would have severely limited U.S. companies in the exporting of both technology and capital. For a while this legislation appeared to command wide support, with strong labor backing. Eventually it was defeated, in part through the efforts of Business International (BI), whose ongoing studies (see Appendix) have helped debunk the charges that overseas investment loses jobs. These BI studies and a number of other research projects document overwhelmingly that foreign direct investment is a win-win proposition, with both home and host countries benefiting.

MNCs clearly have the potential to make a strong, constructive contribution in the struggle to meet human needs and expectations as the world moves into the 1980s. With virtually every country in the world struggling to hold down inflation, and people everywhere demanding more goods and services, the demonstrated capacity of MNCs to increase productivity is desperately needed. Nevertheless, the controversy continues and MNCs remain under fire around the world.

Such attacks on MNCs are, of course, different only in degree from the continuing criticism of the private-enterprise system itself. The intensity of the attack is greater when MNCs are concerned, for the foreign element comes into the picture and accentuates critical feelings. Such adverse public attitudes make a new set of demands on management. This calls for a completely new dimension of management that directs itself to public policy, reaching out to stakeholders, including employees, shareholders, suppliers, local communities, and the public at large.

I believe that management must pay attention to serving as a public advocate for the private-enterprise system and explaining what its company is doing and why, in a comfortable and sure-footed manner. Such responsibilities are as important, and must have as much stress from management all the way up and down the line, as the more traditional responsibilities of organization, personnel, planning, and finance. Where MNCs are concerned, the company's public policy must reach its subsidiaries around the world. Corporate headquarters formulates philosophies and policies responsive to the irreversible movements around the world today (consumerism, industrial democracy, environmental protection, product safety, to name a few), but the policy must be carried out at the local level and requires involvement of local line managers. Operationally this is proving to be very difficult, and with a few exceptions the management methods now being used to move public policy into the field are not very advanced.

Business International in 1979 completed a global study on managing multinational issues sponsored by, and with the active support of, 40 MNCs located all over the world. It was followed by a second global study, "Beyond Money," which examined what various companies were doing in terms of community activities to reach the special needs of the people living where the subsidiaries are located. Out of these two studies BI developed a very interesting and useful country impact-needs audit, which includes a series of questions companies can ask their subsidiary management or use as a discussion guide at meetings with local managers. It also includes a suggested balance sheet generating a body of financial and nonfinancial information designed to quantify a company's contributions to its host country's economy and quality of life. One of the sections of this form is specifically devoted to philanthropic activities.

There is indeed a second bottom line. It calls for a completely new dimension of management, starting with the chief executive officer and permeating the entire organization, reaching subsidiaries all over the world. It demands an understanding of the changing sociology of business and the complex psychology of managing people who are increasingly better educated and independent, more skeptical than obedient. The skills to be public advocate for the company and a sensitive exponent of the private-enterprise system are required. The public's demands for accountability on many fronts must be understood, if not always welcomed.

At Business International considerable thought has been given to the area in which the flexibility of MNCs can come into play in the development effort. Five principles have been identified in which new patterns of partnership between the MNCs and developing countries can—and should be—designed. The five are:

• Investment by MNCs in developing countries must be based on a kind of social compact, if it is to have a real chance of success for both the company and the country.
• The developing country and its government on the one hand and the MNC on the other—both its local managment and its top, parent management—must recognize the basic mutuality of interest in the specific investment.
• To implement the social compact between the MNC and the developing host country, it is important to establish and communicate clearly as many basic objectives, rules, and expectations on both sides as is reasonably possible.
• This includes, but goes well beyond, such factors as the intention, on the part of the MNC, to obey the laws of the host country and act as a good corporate citizen; and on the part of the host government, to support private investment activity. Goals and priorities, both national and corporate, should be defined as clearly as possible, quantified where possible, and communicated in as much detail as possible. Periodic discussions should be held, pinpointing how each partner to the social compact contributes to the objectives of the other partner, as well as to shared objectives. Rules and regulations should be established, agreed upon, and applied clearly and reasonably. Machinery, procedures, and meth-

ods to effect changes in the established ways of doing things should be available to both sides.

- Time periods of the compact should be explicitly examined. Agreements for specific undertakings could be open-ended or have a definite period of applicability, after which conditions can be reviewed or renegotiated. It is only fair to both sides, however, that each be able to count on a given arrangement for a specific, or at least minimum period of time, rather than face abrupt, unexpected alterations.

Management today, more than ever before, is as much an art as a science. Intuitive judgment is as important as computer analysis. Perhaps it all adds up to old-fashioned people-to-people leadership that rests on understanding the human relationships in the system from beginning to end.

5

Communication: Key to Corporate Survival

In this chapter Mr. Freeman pinpoints a major problem for executives: they are not generally prepared to explain business in terms of its values. He contends that unless they do become adept at explaining and defending the system and their companies' contribution to society, the survival of their institutions will be threatened. This chapter, which is based on a presentation made by Mr. Freeman to the National Account Marketing Association in New York in September 1976, is a primer on the corporation's stakeholders, its critics, and the basis of their opposition. It also suggests some ways of dealing with criticism.

Corporate communication is a "political" matter. I know this is a startling assertion that easily leads to misinterpretation or distortion. It is political in the sense of being responsive to constituencies and deriving legitimacy from that responsiveness. Such legitimacy and survival are synonymous, certainly so in the long pull.

I have served in both the political and the business worlds, and some fundamental parallels seem clear to me. In politics the basic task is to create and maintain a system, a society, a world that is free and open enough to make possible individual creativity and fulfillment. In business the need is for a market system free enough to permit private enterprise with all its dynamic attributes and responsive enough to meet the complex, changing, and growing requirements of society.

In a free society business and society have a contract, unwritten but nevertheless enforceable. It requires of society ground rules under which business can work and flourish, and requires from business actions and reactions that are beneficial to society. As a Latin American economist put it, "There can be no economic welfare without social welfare and there can be no social welfare without economic welfare." I concur. The world is moving rapidly toward this recognition's becoming universal.

In such a world perception is crucial. What matters is not only what business does, but what it is believed to be doing. The problem is that business is not accustomed to explaining itself in terms of values. It is experienced and adroit in marketing its goods and services. It is neither experienced nor adroit in selling the values that animate it and that it contributes to society. As one chief executive officer remarked to me, "We are doers, not expositors. That's why we are where we are." The statement is perceptive and accurate, but while true, this cannot continue to be the case, since survival of the corporation itself is at risk.

The Major Corporate Constituencies

There are at least half a dozen constituencies with which business must communicate in new and often changing ways. Let me name them and then sketch some of the issues that revolve around them.

First, employees. I am not referring to the kinds of issues that are negotiated with unions in the collective bargaining process, nor the intricate art of motivating management to make the most creative and dynamic contribution of which it is capable. My concern is the more fundamental challenges with which business must come to terms. My concern is with the growing trend toward greater participation by employees at all levels in the decision-making process, and the parallel trend toward greater participation by employees in the profit of corporate enterprise. It is also focused on the increasing demand for a reorganization of the workplace—the design of that workplace not to meet the requirements of productive machines but to custom tailor it to the needs of productive human beings.

In this redesign of the workplace, there is a special need for companies to come to terms with segments of human resources that have been either misused or underutilized until now: minorities of every kind—the handicapped, racial and ethnic minorities, the very young, the aged—and, of course, women. Imagination and flexibility will be required in designing the workplace so that it can make optimum use of human resources that in the past it has often slighted rather than encouraged. Responding to these vital business constituencies will require acute perception and subtle communication.

Second, consumers. Ralph Nader has made the point more effectively than I could. Business must police itself in the quality of the goods and services it offers and in what it claims for these goods and services. If it does not, other elements of society will. Only corporate responsibility for quality and claims can forestall regulation; only responsiveness to consumers can prevent crippling restraints.

Third, environmentalists. I am not one who believes that economic growth and the protection of the environment are mutually exclusive. Both are possible and both are needed. Some of the claims of environmentalists are extreme and their voices are often shrill. But it is true that business has not in the past considered clean air and clean water as assets that have their own price and must be figured into the cost of a venture along with labor, raw materials, and brick and mortar. I believe that astute executives everywhere understand this now, and figure it into their corporate calculations. But they have not yet succeeded—or have not even tried very hard—in communicating the fact that they do understand and accept that a clean environment is an asset companies must protect and preserve.

Fourth, suppliers. Companies do, of course, keep close track of suppliers in the practical, traditional definition of who and what a supplier is and should be. But how much corporate thought goes to suppliers in the basic, long-term sense, and to the needs and demands of such suppliers, especially when they produce raw materials and commodities in developing countries? Above all, how much corporate thought goes into communicating with these suppliers in a way that makes sense to all concerned? Obviously I don't have very much that is favorable to say for the cartel tactics of OPEC. But something drove the oil countries into joining together the way they did, and is now driving other raw material producers toward similar acts. At the U.N. Commission on Trade and Development meeting in Nairobi in 1976, a Venezuelan delegate—not, mind you, a radical Arab, but the delegate from a democratic country in the Western Hemisphere—served notice that sooner or later the developing supplier countries will corner the market in other raw materials—he cited bauxite and copper—and manipulate it in the same way, and for the same purpose, that OPEC is manipulating oil.

When you ask yourself why, since obviously such tactics are finally destructive to all, the answer is, once again; lack of communication. Companies that are so inventive, efficient, and effective in finding raw materials, getting them out of the ground and processing them, and marketing them have traditionally been unimaginative, insensitive, and demonstrably ineffective in communicating their own worth and values to the supplier societies in which they operate—with results that nearly wrenched the world economy out of shape once, and may finally do so.

Fifth, international organizations. It is the voice of these long-term suppliers that is now heard with insistent repetitiveness in a wide range of international organizations. In the absence of effective corporate communications with these suppliers and these organizations, an atmosphere has been created that has driven companies—and the entire private-enterprise, free-market system—into a posture of defensiveness. The posture is unwarranted, given the vital and constructive role that private enterprise and the free-market system play in economic development. It is also dangerous—not only to corporate survival but also to the welfare, dignity, and survival of mankind.

I do not believe that enforceable legislation, or even effective international regulation, will emerge in the foreseeable future from the rhetorical fireworks that now bedazzle most international organizations and many international institutions. The very voices that so stridently advocate radical change are also the ones that most jealously cleave to the shibboleths of sovereignty and nationalism in their most power-obsessed versions. They are not likely to yield much of either sovereignty or nationalism to achieve even clearly desirable international goals, at least not in the short or medium term. But what they will do, and have already succeeded in doing, is create an atmosphere in which the good faith of business, of all private enterprise, is questioned at every turn and the effectiveness of companies is undermined to a point where the game is not worth the candle. The result of this orchestrated obstructionism is that companies that did such a dynamic job in reaching out for development and growth are driven to abandon the risks and rewards of this kind of venturing, a retreat that can only hold diminishing returns for all.

Sixth, corporate critics. Destructive criticism of this kind—in contrast with constructive criticism, and the socially warranted checks and balances that private enterprise in general and companies in particular need and should welcome—has eddied out from international forums to almost every other segment of society that is involved in setting and disseminating values. Much of academe is on that bandwagon, as are many of the media: print, broadcast, or television. The arts, which once both celebrated and criticized the world and values of private enterprise, are now almost solidly arrayed in opposition. Not surprisingly, public opinion is at best skeptical of business, and more often disdainful or antagonistic.

I recently saw a poll that measured the public view of multinational corporations, not in developing countries, not in controlled market economies, but in western Europe. It showed that in France and Italy 85 percent of the people polled were either "critical" or "very critical" of multinational corporations. It also turned up the interesting fact that people were less critical of multinational companies in countries with labor or social-democratic governments than they were in countries with more conservative regimes. Specifically, the figures for popular distrust of multinational corporations were substantially lower in Great Britain and West Germany than they were in Italy and France. I have a theory as to why this is so. The multinational corporation, aside from being the workhorse of the world, is also a fundamentally revolutionary force, in the sense of turning around a society and moving it in the direction of the future. The society in this instance is human society as a whole, and multinational corporations are moving it in the direction of true internationalization. The international marketplace is, I am convinced, the precursor, as well as the indispensable underpinning, of the global village that now exists in the imagination of futurists, in the political rhetoric of international organizations, and in the real world of multinational companies.

The poll brought up five issues. The first was "International companies are so powerful they are above the law." This is, of course, not true, as any harassed chief executive officer—haunted and hamstrung by the laws, regulations, requirements, and often irrational and contradictory demands of the national sovereignties in which the company operates—will tell you. As one such executive put it to me, "An island with 350,000 people that calls itself a sovereign state can expropriate a subsidiary of General Motors."

Nevertheless, the perception of power is undoubtedly at the core of all antagonism against the multinational company. It is coupled with a suspicion that this power is not exercised in response to society at large, and fused with a resentment against what is seen as the lack of accountability by the multinational corporation. From this I deduce that one of the most important tasks multinational companies must undertake is to communicate to the general public how responsive and accountable they in fact are.

The four other issues revealed by the poll as troubling popular critics of the multinational company all revolve around the same basic concerns:

—"Multinational companies are not concerned with the interests of the countries where they operate."

—"Multinational companies take more out of the countries where they operate than they put in."

—"Multinational companies should be more strictly controlled."

—"The growth of multinational companies tends to lead to monopolies and price fixing."

All of these perceptions have to do with power, with responsiveness, with accountability.

Such perceptions are even more acute in developing countries, where they are coupled with passions that are an amalgam of newly discovered or rediscovered national identity; of a sense of outrage, however unwarranted, over past exploitation or deficiencies; and, most important, of an ambition to change the world and its ways as quickly and as drastically as possible. Hundreds of millions of people in the developing world feel that they have no stake in the global system as it functions at present or has functioned in the past. And the less stake they feel they have, the more radical their desire for change. The change they have in mind may not be reasonable, but the desire for it is understandable and must be addressed.

At Business International we have thought hard about what can be done to bridge the gap in perception. We see disturbing evidence that unless it is bridged, the best intentions and the most competent capabilities can be swallowed up in the chasm. And when we let our imagination run to the extreme possibilities inherent in the current state of affairs, we see not only a $750 billion misunderstanding, but the explosion that is inevitable when passion and power collide. Driven by this vision, we have come up with some ideas for constructing the bridge. They range from the subtle and complex area of perceptions to strategies of communication.

In the realm of perception, multinational companies have to face the fact that however unreasonable or undesirable it may seem, national sovereignties will be with us for a long time and will have to be regarded as partners in economic development and growth—not, as many of us would prefer, as umpires or neutral parties. The realistic choice is increasingly a productive partnership or the destructive sparring of adversaries. This is true everywhere, but particularly and more acutely in the developing world, which in some ways needs most what the multinational company has to offer.

I believe that we must understand, if not necessarily condone, the passion of these critics, and that we must harness their ambition to goals that are beneficial to all. In substance, this means that we must learn to negotiate in a new way, keeping in mind not only the requirements of our companies but also the needs of the country in which we set up a plant, exploit a natural resource, or even sell a turnkey installation. These needs rarely are mutually exclusive. The art lies in finding the terms that most adequately meet the requirements of both partners. And it is a partnership we are negotiating. Imagination is required to see this, and both imagination and flexibility are needed to devise an effective response. In practical terms, companies must learn to "unbundle," to move away from the classic idea and the traditional package of equity, technology, and management, and to offer whatever part of the package is wanted by the host-country "customer."

The complete package is the most effective development tool the world has ever seen, and fragmentation may well weaken its impact. But there is the proverbial horse that you can lead to water but cannot force to drink. And if the host countries now feel that their needs are better served by a part of the package than by all of it, then companies can, and should, respond to that need. The possibilities of profitable response are wide-ranging. The forms of profitable response are as multiple and individual as the combined soundness and imagination of the partners that design them.

At Business International we believe that good corporate citizenship is a fairly simple concept that can be expressed precisely and practiced soundly. We have distilled it into four action points:

—To prove by the company's actions the overall value of its business operation in each country in which it is active.
—To conduct the business of each subsidiary with concern for the national economy of the host country.
—To maintain communications with the authorities and the opinion groups of each country.
—To recognize local regulations, traditions, and practices in employee relations, and to provide opportunities for local technicians, professionals, and executives.

Two tools can translate concept into execution, an execution that is understood and appreciated by both partners. The first tool is the "social audit," which defines the company's social concerns and measures how those concerns are being met as an integral part of the company's activity. A number of international companies have already instituted social audits, each tailored to the company's activities and the social environment in which it operates. Mitsui's social audit, for example, is quite different from British Oxygen's, and both are different from Union Carbide's or from Caterpillar's.

Caterpillar has expressed its social policies in the form of a sound and comprehensive corporate code of conduct, and we believe the formulation of such codes of conduct to be an extremely useful exercise. They make companies aware of their policies and practices, and set the tone and define the assumptions that can then be translated into the mechanism of a social audit. There is nothing wrong with presenting the social audit in a company's annual report. I know of at least one firm that is already doing this, with excellent response from its home government, its employees, and its stockholders.

The other tool in formulating and communicating corporate citizenship is the "corporate balance sheet," which spells out in quantitative terms just what a company contributes to the economy of a host country. Clark Equipment Company, for example, issues such a corporate balance sheet once a year, covering all of its international activities. The balance sheet specifies, in figures, exactly what the company's contribution is to an array of host governments: in terms of employment, which includes figures for salaries and training costs; in terms of strengthening the local economy, which includes such items as taxes, import duties, purchases from local suppliers, and credit granted to local suppliers; and in terms of the national balance of payments. Clark's balance sheet does not ignore or obscure the negative items, including the much-cited payments for technology transfers or the remittance of dividends. Nevertheless, the bottom line makes it unarguably evident that the operations of the company constitute a clear gain to the host country and are profitable to the company and its stockholders as well.

This, in my judgment, is the bottom line of the entire issue. The activities of business, and particularly the activities of multinational companies, with their special dynamic deriving from the ability to make use of the economic principle of comparative advantage in its modern sense, create a win-win proposition. The challenge lies in giving this win-win proposition a form that pleases both sides and in communicating the harmony that such a symmetrical equation holds. I am convinced that it can be done. And the time has come to put our minds to doing it.

6
Questionable Corporate Payments Abroad

The following is based on an unpublished article written by the author and Ms. Ruth Karen. It is a thorough review of the questionable payments issue, with detailed examples of the kinds of problems businessmen encounter in how to handle requests for bribes, implicit or explicit. Mr. Freeman maintains that companies do not make a practice of offering illicit payments, but that they are forced into doing so.

One of the most persistent attacks against multinational corporations centers on the issue of bribery. The charge is that companies corrupt local officials in order to gain access to a market or keep out potential competition. Business International conducted a thorough study of the issue. We found that nothing could be further from the truth than these allegations. Bribery, when it occurs, is a procedure that companies dislike and over which they have little control. Four salient points emerged from our study. Each contradicts currently popular mythology about international corporations.

The first point is that "questionable payments" do not constitute aberrant behavior by some large firms that have suddenly and inexplicably gone haywire. The study shows that the payments follow deeply etched patterns that, to an objective observer, are as unmistakable as ski tracks in fresh-fallen snow. The patterns are a composition of host-country practice, home-country policy, industry characteristics, special factors such as a company's market position or the technology content of its product, and corporate attitude and style. Host-country practice emerged by far as the most important component.

The second point that emerged from the study is that the lion's share of questionable corporate payments abroad are a matter of extortion, not bribery. Payments are demanded—with the demand often accompanied by considerable duress—not offered.

The third point is that companies, with rare exceptions, detest the practice—not only for complex moral or evanescent ethical reasons, but for practical, hard-headed operational reasons. As one executive put it, with both exasperation and conviction: "It's just no way to run a railroad." More pointedly, another chief executive officer noted: "If business is based on payoffs, you can finally go out of your mind because you lose control."

The fourth point is that despite widely held beliefs of the "global reach" persuasion and the passionate contentions of the developing countries, in real life the corporate reach of even the most powerful and efficient international company is limited. Effective influence on joint-venture partners, licensees, distributors, dealers, agents, representatives, consultants, and persons rendering professional services abroad is at best incomplete, and more often very tenuous indeed.

Payments Fall into Three Categories

The study found that major payments ($100,000 and up) tend to be industry-specific as well as host-country-specific, involving typically the aircraft, construction, and communications industries and, in a somewhat different context, turnkey installations, automotive assembly, large sales of capital equipment, and substantial purchases of raw materials. Major payments can also be at stake in the areas of tax assessment and political contributions, whether the latter are legal and disclosed or illegal and undisclosed.

Medium-size payments ($5,000-$100,000) are determined to some extent by such product characteristics as technology content, market position, sourcing alternatives, and profit margins, but in the main are set by commercial custom in the host country. They involve quantity sales of industrial or consumer products to governments or parastate agencies (such as the sale of pharmaceuticals to social security systems, medical instruments to public-sector hospital chains, industrial components to state industries) where the purchasing agent demands a fixed percentage of the sale.

The percentage is usually set by local custom and is not negotiable. In a number of countries, an additional percentage of the sales amount is demanded by another category of public employee to secure or facilitate the collection of receivables from government agencies or parastate institutions. In some countries comparable practices exist in the private sector as well.

Minor payments (under $5,000) are pervasive throughout the developing world. These minor payments are made to low-level and middle-level public employees for such services as clearing goods through customs; securing import or export licenses, work or residence permits, entry or exit papers; and, in some countries, obtaining accommodation, transportation, or communications facilities. Variously described as "baksheesh," "mordida," "dash," or "grease," these are essentially facilitative payments for small but sensitive services rendered.

Major Payments: How and Why

Major payments can be made directly to top levels of the host government and/or political parties in the host country. More frequently they take the form of excessive commissions to agents or representatives, who distribute a portion of the commissions to senior or upper-middle-level employees in a position to approve or veto, facilitate or delay purchasing decisions involving big-ticket items.

Direct payments can consist of crisp bills in elegant envelopes discreetly handed over in an office or at a carefully orchestrated social occasion. More often the method is a credit advance through regular banking channels to the account of an offshore fund, sometimes disguised as a foundation, controlled by the ruler of the host country or members of his family and/or his senior official family. Direct payments of major magnitude are also made to numbered accounts in Switzerland. Surprisingly such transactions have as recipients even top officials in the state trading organizations of the USSR and the other nonmarket economies of eastern Europe. Some host countries have an unwritten code setting out the scale of such payments and the people "entitled" to receive them. That code also provides that if a "qualified" recipient requests payments exceeding the scale, a jail term may be imposed.

Indirect payments are more complex because they involve a legitimate business service rendered, or even an array of business services. For example, the sale of commercial planes to the Middle East at present involves commission payments of about 12 percent if the aircraft company does not have to arrange the financing. If the company arranges the financing, which carries an interest rate averaging 6-6.5 percent, the commission is about 6 percent, for a total of more than 12 percent. The 12 percent commission paid to a local agent therefore includes (a) his acting as a door-opener for the sale and supplying some type of supporting services in the course of negotiations (at minimum this will include providing logistical support—accommodation, transportation, communications, translation, secretarial help—which, in some countries, constitutes an important convenience) and (b) his either making the financing arrangements or being instrumental in making them. Nevertheless, a portion of the commission invariably goes to government officials of the host country at various levels.

This kind of indirect questionable payment is further complicated by the fact that some countries of the Middle East stipulate by law that sales to the country can be made only through a local agent, even if that agent does nothing except sign a paper, which is quite frequently the case. Kuwait, for example, has such a law and has a legally set fee scale for agents. Whether these agents do or do not render any business services to earn their commissions is a problem facing all companies doing business in Kuwait.

Saudi Arabia, too, requires local agents for all business transactions, whether such agents render a legitimate business service or not. One company pointed out that in Saudi Arabia the government's stated reason is that it wants a person physically present in Saudi Arabia over whom it has legal jurisdiction in case problems develop and the government needs recourse. Several firms commented that unofficially the thinly staffed Saudi government uses these agents as a kind of screening mechanism to investigate the many companies that are interested in the Saudi market. It is the Saudis' view that this screening function should be paid for by the companies. Since Saudi Arabia clearly is a buyer's market now and for the foreseeable future, the country is in a position to make this practice prevail in its dealings with companies.

Some companies try to get the maximum amount of legitimate business service for such commissions, and a few succeed to varying degrees. One U.S.-based company, a major manufacturer of capital goods of world repute, is attempting to handle the problem with a detailed schedule of commission payments precisely geared to specific business services rendered by its dealers/distributors, wherever they are.

Another problem connected with this type of commission is that agents and representatives in some countries frequently request that part of the commission be paid outside the home country, usually into a numbered account in Switzerland. In the past most companies went along with this request (the general attitude being "It's his money; he is entitled to do with it as he pleases."), but recently questions have been raised, usually by corporate counsel, whether companies that meet such requests are not, in effect, abetting these agents in avoiding either exchange regulations or fiscal obligations in the host country.

Medium-sized Payments: To Whom and What For

In some countries of Latin America and the Caribbean, it is standard operating procedure for purchasing agents in the public sector to get 3-7 percent of any quantity sale for their private account. Such payment is made in the host country in local currency; in a New York or Swiss bank in U.S. dollars or Swiss francs; or, most frequently, as a split payment, with part delivered in cash in the host country and the remainder deposited in the purchasing agent's name in New York or in a numbered account in Switzerland.

Companies book such payments as commissions, or as sales and promotional expenses, which is what they are. Another way the problem is handled is to appoint a host-country sales agent whose profit margin is large enough to take care of these payments. International companies that have wholly owned sales companies in such countries frequently handle the situation by appointing a host-country national as marketing manager, and giving him either a large enough salary or a large enough expense account to cover this type of payment. Others use a well-paid government-relations man, who fulfills essentially the same function. If the amounts are not too large, his expenses are booked as travel and entertainment. Some U.S.-based companies are beginning to find the problem so intricate and/or risky, and the resulting profit margin so inadequate, that they are considering abandoning these markets, especially if the markets are either small in themselves or marginal to the company's worldwide activities.

What can happen to companies who try to fight the system is

illustrated by the experience of a Swedish firm that lost a sale in one Latin American country because it refused to pay the requested 5 percent of the sales price to a government purchasing agent. A competitor agreed to make the payment. The Swedish firm went to court. In court the prosecutor "lost" the proof the company had provided. The local manager's life was threatened. And the case finally just petered out in the local legal system.

In a number of Asian countries a similar system prevails, especially when the industry or service sector concerned is a government monopoly. The system is also prevalent in some countries of southern Europe, and in at least one country it operates in the private sector as well. In that country, when approached by a purchasing agent for a large private-sector manufacturer for "his" percentage of a sale, the selling firm went to the man's superior to complain. That executive made it clear that he knew all about his purchasing agent's activities, that this was simply the way things worked in the country, and that the calculation of the money involved was, in fact, built into the purchasing agent's salary. In the same country one company that refused to go along with the system found that the expense of breaking into the market without paying off purchasing agents raised its effective marketing cost by 500 percent.

In the Middle East the process is not just accepted, but institutionalized by either law or custom. Typically one company reports that when its agent, accompanied by a visiting headquarters executive, finally managed to get into a government installation to collect an overdue account, the manager of the installation deducted a percentage of the bill for what he described as "the requisite distribution."

Some vital government services can also constitute, or add up to, medium-size payments. The classic case is customs, where what is at stake can be a tariff classification, the release of raw materials or components for an ongoing operation, or the release of perishable goods.

The tariff classification problem is illustrated by a company in a Latin American country with operations that required the importation of industrial diamonds. As a matter of routine, the customs agent classified the diamonds as jewelry, which carried a tariff 300 percent higher. As a matter of routine, the company negotiated for the proper classification, for a sum paid to the customs agent.

There are dangers to this kind of acquiescence. In another Latin American country the general manager of a subsidiary found that a government change also brought a change of senior customs officials, at least of the customs officials with whom that company had dealt. The new man threatened to expose the arrangements made with his predecessor unless he was paid $50,000 to keep quiet. Since there was no way of booking such an expense, the manager started to juggle the subsidiary's books. In the course of an investigation by the parent company, this was discovered. The manager was moved out of the country, and very soon thereafter left the company.

In at least one Latin American country the practice of paying off customs agents for the proper classification or prompt clearance of industrial imports is so prevalent that companies routinely set up special accounts to cover the expense. These accounts are known as "the black box," and the money comes from overbillings by service agencies, such as advertising agencies, public relations organizations, consultants, or even local lawyers, with the difference between service given and service billed going into the "black box."

In another Latin American country there exist organizations whose sole business it is to sell fake invoices for goods or services. Companies enter these invoices into their books and use the money to make the required payoffs to customs agents and to other government employees requesting payments that cannot be covered by normal corporate accounting.

There are ways to fight the system, but they are complicated and require a very special situation. One company, long- and well-established in a Latin American country, was faced with a shipment of components being held up in customs for a payoff. The holdup led to a plant shutdown. The company, which had good labor relations, called in the union and told the local labor leaders what its problem was. The union picketed the customhouse. The goods were promptly released.

But unions can be a problem as well as a help. In a number of Latin American and Asian countries, some union leaders operate close to the margin of banditry, using not only threats of strikes but also threats of arson and/or personal injury to executives and their families to collect payoffs that can run into thousands and tens of thousands of dollars.

Men with comparable power—if a somewhat different style—are plant inspectors who, in some countries, have almost a set scale for rendering the required reports. Inspection and real conditions at the plant have little to do with what goes into the reports.

Minor Payments: More Questions Than Answers

Even companies and countries determined to be "squeaky clean" are convinced that minor facilitative payments are too deeply embedded in local cultures to be eradicable in the foreseeable future. This presents firms with operational questions that are not easy to answer:

—The host country has a price-control mechanism. Applications for price increases are handled by a local trade association or are expedited by its endorsement. To process the application, the association requires a sizable "membership fee." It is generally known that a large part of this membership is spread among the bureaucrats of the price-control agency or, in some countries, goes to the coffers of the governing political party. Should the company fight the system? Can it?

—The household goods of an expatriate executive and his family arrive at the docks. Customs officials want $1,500 to clear them speedily (the goods are supposed to come in duty-free). Delay in clearance means expensive company-paid hotel bills, in addition to discomfort and unhappiness for the executive and his family. Paying the customs official is clearly more cost-effective as well as more convenient for all concerned. Does the company say "no"? Should it?

—An important industrial component or piece of equipment arrives at the host-country air terminal. It takes extra payment to clear it quickly through customs. If it is not cleared quickly, it will (a) delay a production process and (b) accumulate warehousing charges higher than the payment requested. What is the desirable course?

—A company ship comes into port at night. It costs the company $2 million a month to operate the vessel, and the quickest possible turnaround time is important. The company makes arrangements for the required government personnel to work overtime to clear the vessel as soon as it arrives, and pays their overtime. The host government has no funds for overtime compensation. Is this a questionable payment that should not be made?

—A company needs a telephone in a country severely deficient in communications infrastructure. It is asked for $5,000 to get a phone for which the official charge is $25. It might take up to a year to get a telephone without making the requested payment. One company handled that situation by making the payment, then deducting it from its phone bills until the $5,000 "down payment" had been absorbed. As a result the company's line suffered all kinds of interruptions due to a series of inexplicable "mechanical problems." Was that a good procedure?

—The host country requires a tax clearance from an expatriate executive leaving the country. The standard "fee"—what the agent who issues the clearance asks for himself—is $200. One executive, still unfamilar with local custom, responded: "Look, I don't have time to monkey around with your shenanigans. I have to be in the United States within 72 hours for an important meeting." The agent's response: "In that case, it will cost you $300." Since the executive could not leave without the clearance, he finally paid the $300. Did he have a realistic alternative?

—Processing of import licenses, residence permits, work permits, and other routine paperwork is necessary to company operations. In some countries the junior or middle-level bureaucrats handling such papers have worked out a fee schedule for processing them, and give service for the money. In other countries the fees are negotiable. The cost per transaction is somewhere between $100 and $500. The transactions are vital to company operations. Can any company effectively fight such a prevalent system?

—Companies dealing with officials from eastern Europe find that the purchasing agents of the state trading organizations, or their technical advisers, usually arrive in Vienna, Paris, or Stockholm with scanty funds. At minimum companies pay for the hotels, meals, and transportation of these officials. Frequently gifts are called for as well. These can range from television sets or home appliances for the individual official to subscriptions to technical journals for the group. They can include very lavish entertainment. One company, meeting an east European delegation at the Paris airport in order to take the group to inspect the firm's plant in Marseilles, from which the delegation planned to make a major purchase, was asked to change the travel plans. The delegation requested that it be taken not to Marseilles, but to Cannes for an extended weekend. By the time that particular delegation was back on its plane, the cost to the company came close to $10,000. At what point should it have—could it have—said "nyet"?

—The wife of the host-country head of state has a favorite charity that is perfectly valid and legitimate. The company is asked for a donation in an amount exceeding the sum the company customarily sets aside for this kind of contribution. Should the company refuse? Give its customary amount? Alter its contributions list? Enlarge it?

—An international medical society, association of medical technicians, or nursing organization arranges a meeting at which the latest developments and techniques in the field are discussed. Doctors, technicians, or nurses in many countries cannot get funds from their governments or their hospitals to attend these meetings, nor can they afford to pay the cost out of their own pockets. Companies making the medical instruments, medical gases, or pharmaceuticals with which these professionals work want them to be informed on the state of their art. At minimum it means that they will be able to use the companies' products most effectively. The companies pick up the tab for these professionals. One company charters a plane to take professionals to the meeting and return them home. Companies charge such an expense to sales or promotional costs. Would it be better if the professionals of countries or institutions that cannot afford to fund such trips did not attend these meetings?

—In some countries of Latin America, the "aguinaldo"—Christmas bonus—is a venerable institution. It involves not only a company's own employees, but also low- and middle-level public officials with whom the company deals on a regular basis. The total bill for Christmas gratuities to such officials can easily come to $5,000 a year and more. Is this a courtesy? A custom? A bribe?

—In Japan gift-giving on numerous occasions, including business occasions, is traditional. Failure to present the proper gift to the proper person on the proper occasion is seen as uncivilized or at least ill-mannered. Such presents can run into money, in the aggregate. Does a company refuse to make them? And if it makes them, how does it book them? They do not constitute "travel and entertainment." Nor do they, strictly speaking, constitute a sales or promotional expense.

—Finally, how should companies respond to such minor rackets as immigration officials who "forget" to affix an entry stamp on an executive's passport or tourist card, so that, when the executive leaves, a colleague can "discover" the missing stamp and, for a $20 bill, correct the problem? Failure to pay certainly means missing a plane and can stretch into a delay lasting 24 hours or more. That is a lot of executive time for $20. Should the $20 be refused?

Management Action Has Three Phases

Trying to cope with the complexities facing them, companies find they have to move in three steps. First, they have to investigate what is really happening in the company, and determine the extent to which questionable practices have crept into the organization. The second step is to set, and effectively disseminate, policy. The third step is to devise effective mechanisms to enforce that policy.

The investigation process calls for inquiries that are both extensive and intensive. Almost inevitably inquiries involve the board of directors, and frequently a special committee of outside directors. Investigation always involves top management and management at headquarters and subsidiaries, usually three layers deep. Inquiries are pursued by a team consisting of outside auditors and inside auditors, outside counsel and corporate counsel. Companies use written questionnaires, personal interviews, or both. Some questionnaires call for specific, detailed replies; others elicit essay-type answers, essentially asking managers worldwide to tell headquarters just what their problems are, how they solved them in the past, and what they feel would be workable ways of dealing with questionable practices.

The inquiry process is not without problems. In some companies interviewed for study, the board of directors and/or top management were genuinely surprised and shocked by what the investigation turned up. In many firms the process created morale problems in executive ranks, especially among managers of subsidiaries, who felt that headquarters had lost trust in them and was curtailing their scope of judgment; that what was being asked of them was operationally impossible; or, in extremes, that a hypocritical headquarters was demanding profit performance while tying their hands with policies that made it impossible to produce the expected profit.

Inescapably the inquiry process is costly in terms of executive time as well as in cash expenditure.

The Matter of Codes

Companies that have dealt with the problem of questionable payments generally have found that the most efficient way to set policy is to encapsulate it in a written code that is emphatically brought to the attention of all executives. What the code contains is a matter of corporate style. Codes range from a few basic declarative principles to a quite detailed set of operational applications. However formulated all codes contain three elements: the ethical, the operational, the financial.

Addressing itself to the ethical component, one company has come up with a particularly succinct formulation:

> In matters relating to company business, employees should place the interests of the company ahead of their own personal interests. They should place the interests of society ahead of those of the company.

The chief executive officer of another company has an interesting personal litmus test of corporate ethics. In the company code bearing his signature, he says:

> As a guide, I might suggest that possibly the best test of adherence to the dictates of conscience for a person with a family might be to think whether you would be happy to tell your spouse and children or other family members the details of the actions you are contemplating.
>
> If you would not want to do so, this company would not want you to take the action.
>
> Another test would be to decide whether you would be willing to appear on television and explain your actions in detail. Or whether you would be willing to explain your action to a group of friends and neighbors.

In a more pointed approach, another company tells its employees that their behavior should be governed by the precept that "the law is a floor. Ethical business conduct should normally exist at a level well above the minimum required by law."

Even more realistic is the attitude of a firm noting that what was sometimes, in some instances, acceptable in the past, is acceptable no longer. "And," that firm adds pointedly, "we don't want, can't afford, to lose good people, or have them wind up in jail because of questionable payments."

Another firm suggests to its employees that corporate ethics, like all other ethics, are really a matter of enlightened self-interest. Ethical conduct keeps the company out of trouble and ensures its solidity and longevity. It also does not hand a weapon to the enemies of multinational companies and free enterprise. This company tells its managers that "while one questionable local transaction may seem insignificant, cumulatively it is important to the company, to multinational companies as an institution, and to free enterprise as a way of life."

Dealing with the operational component, the chief of international operations for a company with a particularly tight-laced approach defined the company's policy and the cost that policy entailed:

> We mean to be, and intend to stay, squeaky clean. We will obey all laws and regulations everywhere we do business, regardless of local practice. This does restrict our business opportunities, and we know it.

Many companies have come to the conclusion that following local practice, or even scrupulously obeying the local law, is not enough if the intent is to run an operationally tight ship. Such companies make clear in their codes that, as far as they are concerned, the law is only a floor for good corporate behavior. As one firm puts it with some candor:

> Laws in some countries may encourage or require business practices which—based on experience elsewhere in the world—we believe to be wasteful or unfair. Under such conditions it scarcely seems sufficient for a business manager to merely say, we obey the law, whatever it may be!

The financial component of a company code is in some ways the easiest to state because it is the most concrete. A substantial number of companies have pulled the financial element into a set of eight injunctions that seem to cover the ground:

—The use of corporate or subsidiary funds or assets for any improper purpose is strictly prohibited.

—No undisclosed or unrecorded fund or asset of the corporation or any subsidiary shall be established for any purpose.

—No false or artificial entries shall be made in the books and records of the corporation or its subsidiaries for any reason, and no employee shall engage in any arrangement that results in such prohibited acts.

—No payment on behalf of the corporation or any of its subsidiaries shall be approved or made with the intention or understanding that any part of such payment is to be used for any purpose other than that described by the documents supporting the payment.

—Any employee having information or knowledge of any unrecorded fund or asset or any prohibited act shall promptly report such matter to the controller and/or auditor or general counsel of the corporation.

—All managers shall be responsible for the enforcement of and compliance with this policy, including necessary distribution to ensure employee knowledge and compliance.

—Appropriate employees will periodically be required to certify compliance with this policy.

—This policy is applicable to the corporation, its divisions, and all its domestic and foreign subsidiaries.

The Limits of Enforcement

Most companies that have formulated or updated their written policies enforce them through a mandatory annual sign-off required from all senior managers at headquarters and in subsidiaries. These sign-offs certify that managers have complied with the spirit as well as the letter of the code. To dot the "i" the chief executive officer makes clear that noncompliance means an end to the executive's career in the firm. This works at headquarters and in domestic operations, but it already has led to some nasty problems in subsidiaries that are wholly or majority owned.

The chief executive officer of one company with extensive operations in the Middle East, Asia, Africa, Latin America, and southern Europe—areas in which questionable payments are generally standard operating procedures—notes:

> Say I write rules and distribute them and leave it at that. It's a waste of time and effort. The local managers just think this is another one of those peculiar U.S. customs and ignore it. They'll believe I mean it only if the directive is backstopped with very stringent controls, financial and managerial. Such controls are very costly and not always possible. And you lose your best local managers by trying to enforce these controls, at least as long as your competitors—U.S., European or Japanese—allow their local managers to operate in the locally customary fashion.

Even more disturbing to companies is that through strict enforcement, they may literally be risking the lives of local managers. Several companies have been told by their local managers in South and Central America and in some Asian countries that if questionable payments become publicly known, the local manager runs the risk of landing in jail, getting beaten up in a dark alley, or even being killed.

But the real limits of enforcement begin with minority joint ventures and apply with increasing tightness to licensees, dealers, distributors, agents, and consultants. In all of these relationships companies have at best a marginal degree of influence and no workable power.

Companies have tried to write their codes into their contracts with licensees, with results that have run the gamut from pro forma compliance to inability to do business in certain countries. Trying to get dealers and distributors to concur in the company's code has produced reactions ranging from appreciation of the company's posture (not necessarily followed by action) to dismissal of the request as either presumptuous or irrelevant. The full complexity of the problem is illustrated by one company with a well-defined corporate code that it enforces successfully at headquarters, in all domestic operations, and in its wholly or majority-owned subsidiaries. But the company noted that it has about 25,000 distributors throughout the world, many of them distributors for its 40-odd subsidiaries.

"Whatever these distributors do comes out of their profit margin," the chief executive officer said. "It would be ludicrous to ask them to sign off on our code. And if they did sign off, it would be meaningless." This is confirmed by the experience of a firm that tried to get a sign-off from its distributor in Indonesia. The man smiled and said: "Of course. Do you want my sign-off on pink paper, white paper, or yellow paper?"

Attempting to enforce codes with agents is an even more improbable endeavor. Companies make the effort by spelling out commercial terms with the greatest possible precision, which presumably leaves no margin for questionable payments, at least of any magnitude. Some firms now ask their agents for written affidavits certifying that the agent has retained any money paid him by the company. Companies find that they can get such affidavits, if they insist, but have no way of knowing how meaningful they are. Often they have good reason to suspect that they are about as meaningful as that Indonesian distributor's sign-off.

Enforcing company codes with consultants is next to impossible. Consultants are independent professionals with their own standards of ethics and behavior. These are in no way subject to corporate control or influence, and the best companies can do in such relationships is to introduce some kind of headquarters control mechanism, usually a financial one. The typical way to exercise control is a requirement that headquarters must approve—before any commitment is made—all fees to consultants, including local counsel, that are not in the normal course of business and/or exceed $1,000 a year.

In dealing with consultants many companies have run into the additional problem of legitimate consultants, rendering legitimate services at a legitimate price, requesting to have all or part of their fees paid outside their home countries. Companies can refuse to do this—and some do refuse—thereby running the risk of losing good professional service. Other companies, reasoning that it is really not their business to tell an independent professional what to do with a fee, comply with whatever method of payment the consultant requests. Most companies walk a wobbly line down the middle, well described by one firm:

> Our policy is to respond to a consultant's request for payments made outside his own country—and we know he may be violating exchange or tax regulations. We feel that we cannot tell an independent professional, rendering a legitimate service, what to do with his money. But we will not pay any funds into a numbered account. The reason we don't do that is for our own protection. We want to make certain that no slush funds develop in this company.

What, Then, Is the Answer?

Given these realities and complexities, what can be done? What should be done? Self-regulation by each company and, to the extent possible, by at least U.S. companies in concert, is undoubtedly the most desirable and effective way to fight this particular system. But that method has limits, some of them described above, and has competitive disadvantages as well.

We have come to the conclusion, therefore, that it is desirable for the U.S. government to take the lead in shoring up corporate defenses with national legislation and, through active and outspoken leadership, to get international regulation. This holds if—and it is an important if—the intent and application of national legislation and international regulation is preventive rather than punitive, and if legislation and regulation are realistic about facilitative payments. The issue of extraterritoriality is sticky and the matter of competition, worrisome. But the basic concern is overriding.

Roderick Hills, chairman of the Securities and Exchange Commission during the mid-1970s when the problem began to make international headlines, notes that "questionable payments threaten to have a corrosive effect on the integrity of our system of capital formation, and defy or circumvent the system of corporate accountability on which U.S. securities laws—and indeed the U.S. system of mass capital formation—rest."

His successor, Harold Marvin Williams, adds:

> In the long run, honesty is not only the best business policy, but the only one compatible with the free market and with open competition. Corruption—whether it involves bribes to secure overseas contracts, illegal contributions to political candidates at home, or hampering the efficient function of the marketplace—results in higher prices, lessened responsiveness to the consumer, and lower quality of goods and services. Business corruption is not only inefficient; it destroys the marketplace.

We concur. The issue goes to the integrity of the international corporation as an institution. Its survival is at stake. Practicality, morality, and good sense all point in one direction: to fight the good fight, and appreciate all allies in the battle—including any government, any international body—that lines up on the same side.

7
Risk and the Future

The following chapter is adapted from the author's remarks at a conference of the Risk Studies Foundation held at New York in September 1978. It explores the risks, both political and economic, that create uncertainties for operating internationally. It starts with the perils of the arms race, but goes well beyond this to include the dangerous predicament of a world in which a large portion of the population lives in poverty and virtual starvation. The latter is considered by the author as a pressing global problem with grave risks for peace.

With the world becoming increasingly complex, there are risks that must be faced and dealt with as best we can, although facing these risks also means acceptance of the fact that much of their management is out of our hands. There is also uncertainty that, given alertness and attention, can be managed. Both should be contrasted with change, which holds new opportunities as well as new dangers, challenge as well as confusion, hope and promise as well as disillusionment and threat.

Major risks fall into two categories—political and economic—although, of course, the two are not separable in real life, and interact everywhere and at all times. The most fundamental risk in political life today is destruction. Perhaps it would be more accurate to say geopolitical life, since that deals with both mankind and the environment.

For the first time in history, mankind has the capacity to destroy itself—not metaphorically, as great artists and religious leaders have warned us through the ages, but literally. We can be dead at any moment if the current balance of terror is tilted by either intent or mistake. It is an awesome thought. But its very dimension makes it unlikely that any country will, as a matter of policy, launch a preemptive strike with nuclear weapons.

I say "as a matter of policy" because there is always the risk of human error and human passion, especially when that passion expresses the desire of what someone has called "the desperate minority." There are such minorities in many places today. Their chosen weapon is terrorism—bloody, promiscuous, and unpredictable. Business International recently conducted an international investigation of the patterns of terrorism, and the policy decisions major multinational companies must make to try to protect themselves—their executives, their employees, their stockholders—from its ravages. The risks that these desperate minorities and their terrorist tactics represent are real. They could set off a chain reaction of passion and counterpassion that might, at some point, become difficult to control. Their existence enlarges the possibility of human error in wielding the nuclear weaponry that lies in our arsenals.

The paramount policy risk we face today emanates from the Soviet Union's commitment to expansion. That commitment has two components. The first is nationalistic. The USSR has a long history of aggrandizement and hegemony, and a strong case can be made that this drive reaches back to the period of the czars and even earlier. The Soviets are simply carrying on, in their own terms, an age-old Russian tradition. The other component of today's Soviet expansionism is the revolutionary, Marxist one: the drive to carry the theology of Marxism—and it is a theology, in its dogma and its evangelic passion—to every corner of the globe, and to be part of every revolutionary movement that frees nations and people—or at least claims to free nations and people—from dominations of the past, whether political, economic, or social.

I haven't had the opportunity to confer on a personal basis with the head of state of the USSR since 1963, when I had a long talk with Nikita Khrushchev at the Kremlin, but I did have a fascinating four-and-a-half-hour conversation with Fidel Castro at Havana that was followed by a four-hour interchange between

Castro and some 75 senior executives whom Business International brought to Havana in November 1977 for what in diplomacy they call a free and frank exchange of views. Under Business International's ground rules, that means an off-the-record, no-holds-barred session, with questions and responses coming hard and fast from both sides. What this encounter in Havana made clear to me is that Castro has a revolutionary commitment to carry the Marxist system to people around the world, whatever it takes. He believes in the system and believes that it will bring a better life to people everywhere, most particularly in the developing countries, where they now suffer a great many deprivations.

The expansionist drive of the USSR—of which Cuba is an integral part—is a danger, and will remain one for some time to come. This is true whether the expansionist motivation is hegemonistic, humanistic, or a combination of the two. The danger lies not only in the nature of this expansion, but also in the reaction it provokes from the free world generally and the United States particularly. The real risk is that the USSR and its satellites will step over a line, and in doing so will trigger a feeling that they must be stopped. There is a strong countervailing force to such a turn of events. Rising nationalism and a sensitivity to interference from the outside tend to reject any intervention, including intervention that is wrapped in the cloak of Marxism. Events in Egypt in the 1970s have demonstrated that. The statements of African leaders at the meeting of nonaligned nations in Belgrade were most emphatic on the same point.

In sum, I believe that while the danger does exist of Soviet imperialism or Marxist evangelism going too far and setting off a reaction that might get out of hand, the chances of this happening are diminishing—at least for the moment.

The real risk is that the arms race, triggered by the two major contesting systems in the world today, will mushroom to such size that it will effectively limit the world's productive capacity for civilian purposes, and hamper the world's ability to meet the basic needs and rising expectations of its people. The arms race, if its dimensions get out of hand, could steer human effort away from the production of goods and services, and their equitable distribution, and create an atmosphere of fear, of scarcity, of an inward-looking defensiveness that would result in a rejection of universalism, a denial of the realities of interdependence, a running for cover in the old shibboleths of protectionism, isolationism, and beggar-thy-neighbor selfishness and delusion. The result of that scenario would be a breakdown of the emerging global economy that has been developing since 1960, and a return to the pattern of the 1930s, with massive depression, unemployment, and human misery that finally led to the pent-up frustrations that exploded in a world war.

Beneath this danger, resulting from a dwindling and increasingly shaky economic base, I perceive another menace more volatile and potentially even more explosive. It is mainly economic, but it is also sociopolitical. It is incredible and indefensible that in a world of real plenty for many, and potential plenty for all, 900 million people should still live in grinding poverty, the kind of poverty in which men, women, and children get up each day and go to bed each night sometimes cold, often unsheltered, and always—I repeat, always—hungry. What makes this fact even more devastating is that today this is a way of life for 150 million more people than eked out an existence in this manner a decade ago. I have seen these people throughout the world, and I know that neither they, nor I, can accept this condition. Something must be done.

When it comes to taking action, experience has shown that quantifying a problem makes a good beginning. In the 1970s per capita income of the developed countries rose about $900, to a total of $4,000 a year. Granted that this figure contains an illusionary element of inflation. Granted also that the per capita figure is an average that does not illuminate the inequities of income distribution that, even in the most advanced industrial countries—whether they are market economies or centrally planned economies—leave pockets of the population insufferably and inexcusably far below that average.

But the figure that really boggles the mind is that in the same period, average per capita income in the poorest of the developing countries—the countries that we now subsume under the innocuous-sounding phrase "the Fourth World"—which contain at least one-quarter of the people on this planet, went up from $105 per year to $108. How long do you think a quarter of the human race will continue to accept this state of affairs?

The answer to that question is already known. The proverbial writing is on the wall, and we of the developed countries, of the industrial world, have been found wanting—and rightly so. In response the developing countries, of both the Third World and the Fourth World, have organized themselves politically. They have formed what is known as the Group of 77, which actually includes well over 100 nations that stand together in the United Nations and all other international confrontations as a cohesive group, with differences that are great but with concerns that override these differences. They demand a new international economic order. And while some of the ingredients of that new order are perhaps wrong-headed and impractical, the basic thrust is, in my judgment, the way the world must go if it is not to explode.

If approached constructively and managed wisely—two very big ifs—solutions are possible that will serve the requirements and meet the aspirations of all parties, not only in a new international economic order but also in a new global bargain that holds the hope, and a reasonable prospect, of liberty and justice for all. Let me outline briefly what I consider to be some basic ingredients of such a solution.

I would begin with the network of international economic organizations and institutions that we have built over the decades, but most particularly and most effectively since the end of World War II. These need to be both widened and strengthened to become more sound and more comprehensive. They must be augmented to include the Third and Fourth Worlds, in a way that not only brings the nations and peoples of these worlds into the network of global economic and financial structures, but also makes them realize that it is in their best interest to become an integral part of these structures.

Planning, persuasion, and perception are involved in translating this possible solution into effective reality. To put it in more practical terms, it is a matter of engineering and communication, of management in the most fundamental and most encompassing meaning of that challenging concept. I have some specific ideas about how this concept of sane, sound, and effective global management can be approached in bite-size pieces, although I would have to agree that the bites are—as indeed they must be—very big bites indeed.

One idea—not original with me, but everything in my own experience tells me that it is a very good one—is the idea of a Marshall Plan funded by the developed world for the developing world (see Chapter 9). It is an idea that is picking up momentum. This new Marshall Plan—and I will refer to it, more accurately in this new context, as the marshalling plan—calls for a concerted, combined effort by the industrialized countries and the OPEC nations to help the countries of the Third and Fourth Worlds build up their agriculture and industry, thereby creating productive opportunities for the unemployed and underemployed of these nations, and turning them into consumers with not only an appetite to purchase but also a purchasing power that will provide vast new markets.

Concurrently this quantum jump in productive power in the developing world would produce goods and services—from vital mineral and energy resources to creature comforts such as coffee, cocoa, and tea at affordable prices; from new approaches to research and development to the rewards of a new brand of tourism that would include genuine people-to-people exchange—that would enrich the lives of the industrial countries in every sense of that word. Barbara Ward, in her precise and elegant terminology, sums up this concept, and this process, as an undertaking that "would allow the rhetoric of interdependence to be turned into a genuine alliance of productive interests."

The political concept that underlies this marshalling plan is linkage. Linkage has assumed some doubtful overtones and undertones as it is bandied about in international relations, but I think it applies soundly and solidly in this economic context, where the chain effects are so clearly visible. The hard fact is that today most of the industrial countries are afflicted by high unemployment, slow growth, and continuing inflation, with more of the same predicted for the foreseeable future. OECD statistics, and the projections based on these statistics, bear this out.

At the same time the developing countries, particularly those in the Fourth World, suffer directly from the repercussions of this recession, and even the countries that have profited wildly from the raising of oil prices have to realize that they are not immune. They, too, have felt the effects of inflation, recession, and the protectionist pressures that stagflation has created in the industrialized world. The linkage of which I speak consists of the recognition that the economy of the world is one chain and, in the final analysis, that chain is no stronger than its weakest link.

The evident answer, therefore, is to strengthen the entire chain by soldering all its connections. In practical terms this means moving toward a more dynamic global economy that will energize productive resources in both the industrial countries and the developing world. That is what the marshalling plan is all about.

Within this overall approach I would like to offer a specific procedure for applying the acetylene torch to a number of connections in the chain that are now weak. It is a procedure I describe as "triangulation," involving three parties: an OPEC country, a developing host country, and a multinational corporation. The procedure I envisage would put together, in a productive package, the surplus capital of an OPEC nation—in excess of $30 billion of such capital is currently generated every year and is looking for productive outlets—the resources, either natural or human, of a developing country, and the expertise and know-how—technological, managerial, marketing—of a multinational corporation. At Business International we believe that this kind of package promises a new investment pattern that will become more popular, more pervasive, and more powerful, simply because it must, by the force of its own logic. It makes good sense all around.

It is—if approached constructively and managed effectively—a self-evident win-win proposition. We intend to address ourselves in a systematic way to the opportunities this win-win proposition offers, the problems it presents, and the procedures that need to be developed to create the best possible package for all parties. We are convinced that it will make an important contribution to reinforcing the global chain of economic links that I have described.

The Character of Change

I would like to say a few words about change. While risk is something we can prepare for, forestall, and, one hopes, cope with, change must be understood. At Business International we are currently engaged in an exercise that is analytical, practical, and, we believe, fundamental. We call it "managing multinational issues." In approaching the task of identifying the issues that need to be managed, we came up against the inescapable need to define the characteristics and dimensions of the changes that lead to the issues that must be addressed.

We have uncovered six major characteristics that are integral to change in our time. The first of these is that change is happening faster than ever before. James Thurber, in his inimitable fashion, offered an image that is marvelously apt: "Man is moving too fast for a world that is round. Soon he will catch up with himself in a great rear-end collision, and will never know that what hit him from behind was man."

The inescapable fact of our lives is that since World War II technology has dominated change. The rate of technological innovation may now be slowing; many predict this, but I consider it far from certain. Even if it were so, changes that have already taken place affect people's lives and lifestyles today, and will do so for decades to come. Technology has telescoped time.

A second characteristic of change is that it is more complex than it has ever been. The reason for this is that by accepted estimates in the scientific community, 90 percent of all scientists ever born are alive today, and are employed in creating change. As a result the complexity and sophistication, let alone multiplicity, of future innovation is likely to challenge the comprehension of even the most informed layman. That will make the world a perhaps more efficient, but certainly a less understandable, place.

A third characteristic of change in our time is that it is increasingly universal. When Abraham Lincoln was assassinated, it took a week for the news to reach the people of the American West. When John F. Kennedy was killed, most of the world had immediate access not only to the information but also pictures of the event.

On the other end of this spectrum of universal experience in our time is the fact that when U.S. astronauts stepped from their space capsule and planted the American flag on the dusty surface of the moon, more than half the people of the world watched this giant step for mankind as it was happening, and most of the rest saw it on film within the subsequent 72 hours.

It is almost a cliché to say that the world has shrunk from the unfathomable center of the universe to the size of a marble we can toy with. Today events in the most remote corner of the planet are not only knowable but can be known in a matter of minutes everywhere else. And the effects of this instant access to human experience everywhere—good or bad, triumphant or disastrous—obviously are not only technological. They are commercial, economic, political, social, and cultural. They reach, and affect for better or worse, in one way or another, virtually all the people of this planet.

A fourth characteristic of change today is that it is more disorienting than it has ever been. All innovation has side effects that are unwanted and unplanned, and the technologies that have made our planet a global village are no exception. Psychologists say that each of us has an internal time metabolism. It is a highly individualized mechanism, and no two are alike. It is defined as the period required to absorb and internalize events and images. Today the rate and dimension of change have exponentially increased the number of events and images with which each of us is presented. But the old institutions, relationships, and societal contexts remain largely unchanged. The result is a psychic indigestion, a kind of societal jet lag, that is as fatiguing and disorienting as is the jet lag experienced when traveling, even when one travels in a comfortable and convenient widebody jumbo plane.

A fifth characteristic of change, distressing in itself and even more distressing because it seems so contradictory to the recognition that we all live in a global village, is that change is more divisive. The divisiveness results from a number of influences, in many cases the same influences that create interdependence and make unification possible. These influences are rising affluence, increasing education, travel, and the instant visual access to experience and events made possible by television. Those who live in the ghettos of the global village, whether in less-developed countries or in the slums of New York, London, or Tokyo, have a pretty good idea of who is getting what in the world. As a result they feel they are being bypassed. Not surprisingly they want their piece of the action, including the luxuries they see others enjoying—and, in keeping with the speed of change, they want it now. Rising expectations combine with widespread dissatisfaction to create a time bomb that is ticking away on the doorsteps of mankind's traditional institutions.

These expectations, and that dissatisfaction, are not limited to basic needs, or to the developing world. The manifestations—both in the industrialized countries and in the developing nations—have one other characteristic. Change is becoming more qualitative and selective, more individually determined, and therefore will take numerous and unpredictable forms. Rising levels of affluence, education, and expectations, though still painfully maldistributed throughout the world, are nevertheless providing hundreds of millions with choices about the kind of world in which they want to live.

What will these choices be? What will they demand of us? How can they be ordered, worked into a structure of global harmony? It is my contention that these questions encapsulate the fundamental risks of our time, and that devising answers to them—answers that work—is the true meaning, and gigantic challenge, of risk management today.

8
Prospects for Government-MNC Relations

In this chapter Mr. Freeman, in looking at the U.S. business climate, maintains that the relationship between government and the private sector is, and must be, adversarial because of the needs for checks and balances of relative powers. The author describes how and why this must be so, but he does recognize that governments can, and often do, overstep their authority, thereby weakening the system. His point of view, which was presented at Business International's 1979 Chief Executive Officers' Roundtable in Kauai, Hawaii, is a controversial one.

The government-private sector relationship can best be described with one word: "adversarial." Relations between governments and private enterprise have always been so, and always will be. We should recognize the fact, understand the reasons, and pattern our activity in interacting with government accordingly. Let me hasten to add, however, that an adversarial relationship between government and the private sector need not be harsh. To be an adversary does not require being antagonistic, deprecatory, supercritical, or totally negative.

The truth is that the adversary relationship between government and private sector can, and should, become a basically healthy one that adds up to a balance of power. That is, the power of the private sector countervailing abuses and shortfalls by government (including multinational companies countervailing the nationalistic abuses of nation-states) and vice versa, with government countervailing the abuse of power by private companies. Perhaps an analogy to the separation of powers in the U.S. government among the executive, the legislative, and the judiciary is valid.

What I am driving at is this: If we understand the nature of the government-private sector relationship and the sources of and reasons for the built-in adversary stance, then government and private business can talk to each other, with an understanding of the role each must play to build a more prosperous and meaningful world.

Permit me a short historical sketch to provide background for the points I will try to make. The philosophy of the market economy and the private-enterprise system rests on Adam Smith's *An Inquiry into the Nature and Causes of the Wealth of Nations*, written in 1776. The essence of Smith's philosophy is that the wealth of a nation results from the diligent pursuit by each citizen of his own self-interest. In serving his own interest, each citizen, Smith concluded, serves best the public interest: "He is guided as though by an unseen hand." "Better," Smith said again and again, "that unseen hand than the visible, inept and predacious hand of the state."

In 1776 the mercantilist system, in which the government controlled everything and the state was the end-all, was completely dominant. The individual entrepreneur was struggling to escape from state control. So the private-enterprise system and the market economy came into being as an adversary force and system, fighting to break away from the government and the state. That adversarial relationship has continued, in a modified form, since then.

At different times and places in history, private enterprise has become almost free of government, but never completely so. Accordingly, it is a misnomer to use the phrase "free enterprise." It is more accurate and descriptive to designate the system as private enterprise in a market economy. The extent and dimension of the freedom from government, never complete, have varied significantly as the adversarial relationship between government and private business has fluctuated.

To understand the interaction and attitudes of government and the private sector, it is useful to trace the three main currents of adversary interaction. They are quite different, and when that difference is understood, the interaction that takes place can be seen as more constructive than is the case when all the actions are lumped together under one label, such as "government interference."

The first current of government-company relationship is regulation. Actually the laissez-faire doctrine of the "invisible hand" and "natural selection" is a very harsh one. Carried to the extremes that David Ricardo, Thomas Malthus and Herbert Spencer carried it in England, and William Graham Sumner and Henry Ward Beecher in the United States, it justified what today would be considered predatory and inhumane practices by almost any businessman. And so a long chain of regulations began.

First came the regulations of working conditions, especially those of women and children; then wages, hours, and pensions; collective bargaining followed; and, most recently, participation and codetermination by workers. Quality and purity of product gradually came under government surveillance. Environmental considerations, with pollution regulations, wax strong today. Trade practices, antitrust and antimonopoly laws and regulations, became important in the twentieth century, as did regulation of securities, finance, and banking.

By its nature and origin this regulatory relationship tends to be highly adversary in nature. The government officials who enforce the regulations, especially if they have never worked in the private sector, tend to consider private companies antisocial. More often than not, they equate profit with selfishness. The regulatory official who recognizes the importance of profit in stimulating productivity, allocating resources, and building capital for growth and expansion is the exception.

Accordingly relations between government and the private sector on the regulatory front are likely to be extremely sensitive. Companies should act accordingly, and not expect much consideration or understanding from the regulators. Care should be taken to avoid violations and to be prepared for tough handling in the event of even inadvertent violation.

Having painted a rather tough adversary picture on the regulatory side, I hasten to add that there is some reason to believe that the regulators are becoming less harsh. For one thing, the size and complexity of economies and companies are such that there is a growing realization, even by the regulators, that rules and regulations have grown so complex that in many cases they are counterproductive, seriously impeding productivity. Nonetheless, where the regulators are concerned, industry should recognize that the relationship with government is, and will continue to be, sharply adversarial in nature.

The second current of government-company relationship is the provision of services to the public: police and fire protection, education, health (particularly preventive medicine), rehabilitation, recreation, welfare, and pensions are some of the government services provided to citizens. For the most part the relationship between private enterprise and government is only mildly adversarial where public services are concerned.

The third current of government-company relationship varies widely in degree and level of the adversarial interchange: government involvement in the economy as a principal party rather than as a regulator. Philosophically the antithesis of Adam Smith and the "unseen hand" of the *Wealth of Nations* is Karl Marx's *Das Kapital* and the *Communist Manifesto*, with its repudiation of competition and private property, which led to the Russian Revolution and the state socialism and centralized, detailed economic planning followed in the USSR today.

In between the extremes of laissez-faire—with no government involvement except minimum regulation—and state socialism, Soviet style, there are many levels of government-private sector economic relationships. They range from government ownership of utilities, manufacturing companies, mines, land, farms, and commodities of various kinds to joint ventures with private companies. Various levels of government planning also take place, from the "indicative planning" practiced in France to "Japan Inc." and the highly successful system followed in South Korea. In the developing world the degree of planning and government involvement tends to run high, not necessarily because that area is Marxist and socialist in philosophy, but because resources, both human and material, are so limited and demands are so great that more government involvement is inevitable.

As far as government involvement in the economy is concerned, the point I wish to make is that in many places the relationship need not be harshly and sharply adversarial. Governments are increasingly coming to the realization that by their very nature they are not unequipped to operate efficiently where the production and distribution of goods are concerned. Since the mid-1970s we have found at Business International Government Roundtables, which give a unique and penetrating insight into how governments think and act, that they are changing to a more positive attitude toward the market economy and private enterprise. Canada, Kenya, Spain, Italy, India, Argentina, and the United States are examples. The same can be said for France, Brazil, Sri Lanka, Japan, South Korea, Mexico, and Nigeria, to name just a few. At the other extreme I can't name a country in the world that admires or really wants to copy verbatim the state socialism practiced by the Soviet Union and the command economies of eastern Europe or the People's Republic of China.

It is my observation that in the contest in the world marketplace, Adam Smith's philosophy of competition and the market economy is slowly prevailing over Karl Marx's philosophy of "from each according to his ability; to each according to his need." I think this is quite extraordinary in a world of instant communication. However, the contest certainly is not over. The market economy and the private-enterprise system could yet break down as the world tries to build the international institutions necessary in a time of great and growing interdependence. The fact that we still think, plan, and act in terms of nation-states instead of globally (and thereby inconsistently with the reality of interdependence) explains why we are in trouble today in the industrial world, with low growth rates, a weak dollar, heavy pressure on natural resources, stagflation, and great uncertainty about, and lack of confidence in, the future.

The major threat for the future is a reversion to mercantilism and statism that will choke the private-enterprise system before the necessary adjustment to the reality of global interdependence can be made. Already we see, particularly in Europe, heavy state intervention in the market economy to prop up noncompetitive sectors and companies and to protect jobs by government action. Far too often such government intervention is made with the concurrence and support of the local private sector. Such ad hoc interference in the marketplace is a major threat to a return to levels of productivity that can check inflation and meet burgeoning human needs. It also triggers retaliatory responses and threatens to provoke a return to protectionism.

We are going through a very difficult and dangerous period. Major changes are necessary as the world and its nation-states adjust to the reality of interdependence. That adjustment within the respective countries is made very difficult by the political pressures created by unemployment during a period of diminished economic growth. The labor movement in country after country, including the United States, has been highly protectionist. This reversion makes it all the more important that the private sector, particularly multinational companies, fight hard to block protectionist government intervention in the economy. It also underscores the need for companies to provide enlightened leadership so that the market economy can remain dynamic and make the adjustments that must be made if progress and human betterment are to continue.

The relation between government and private enterprise must be cooperative; adversarial, to be sure, but not antagonistic and "at war." Signals from the marketplace can continue to point the way to necessary adjustments in a time of great change. However, the adjustments that must be made, such as developing new sources of energy and natural resources and recycling resources, are so massive and capital-intensive that new levels of government-private sector industry cooperation are essential. I believe this process of better accommodation and an enlightened adversarial relationship is slowly taking place, but it must speed up if the market economy is to survive.

9
The Antidote for Worldwide Stagflation: A Global Marshall Plan

In this chapter Mr. Freeman outlines his program for a global Marshall Plan, a theme he has been pressing to corporate and governmental audiences since early 1974. This is extracted from the speech he gave at the World Future Society's meeting at Toronto in 1980. The Global Marshall Plan, or marshalling plan, as Mr. Freeman also likes to refer to it, is that three-way cooperation needed of multinational corporations, OPEC, and developing countries to solve development problems. He believes that the multinational corporation is particularly suited for this task. However, he warns that the development objective will best be accomplished if multinational corporations are not "unbundled" to take just some of the components, as critics would like. He stresses that all of what multinational corporations have to offer is interrelated and important.

As the world stood at the threshold of the 1970s, global business opportunities looked very bright. The decade of the 1960s had had its own traumas, of course. The Vietnam War, and the profound social changes it set in motion, made that decade one of the unhappiest and most disillusioning periods in U.S. history, with echoes that reverberated throughout the Western world. Nevertheless, and perhaps surprisingly, throughout the 1960s, a decade of social unease and political distress, solid economic progress took place in the industrial nations. The annual growth rate generally held at a 5 percent level, and inflation, though troublesome in some countries, was less than 3 percent per year overall. There was virtually full employment—indeed, some countries in western Europe had to import workers in substantial numbers—and the great majority of people had money to buy more and more of the material possessions that are usually described as "the good things of life."

As we moved into the 1970s, there was confidence that intelligent use of Keynesian economic principles would make it possible to fine-tune economies by skillful monetary and fiscal intervention. Recessions and depressions, it was thought, were no longer a real threat. Although the business cycle would continue in its traditional form, it could, and would, be moderated to avoid the damaging and dangerous extremes.

As we now know, those expectations were not fulfilled. In the 1970s growth rates sank to less than 3 percent per year, and there was a menacing shift from the virtually full employment of the 1960s to worrisome unemployment. More distressing still, this serious change in the employment picture of the industrialized nations was accompanied by double-digit inflation that made it dangerous—in fact impossible—to use the classical fiscal and monetary measures to stimulate the economies of the Western world. Equally serious, the situation deeply shook the Western world's confidence in its capacity to manage its affairs and in the ability of the private-enterprise market system to sustain economic growth, provide jobs, and make available the good things of life that people demand in this age of rising expectations.

As one looks back over the 1970s and compares that decade with the 1960s, this loss of confidence is not hard to understand. Not only had the industrial economies performed poorly, but few had been able to foresee the major events that triggered the stagflation that remains with us as we move into the 1980s.

Let me enumerate the salient developments no one really saw coming. No one foresaw the massive worldwide inflation that began even before OPEC accelerated the process. No one foresaw the world grain shortage that occurred in 1972 and 1973.

There was a boom as the global economies took off in 1973 but it was short-lived. Its demise was predicted by only a few, and the expected rolling readjustment forecast for 1974 turned into the severest recession since the Great Depression. The industrial world moved on a treadmill of inflation and recession, producing in the process a new phenomenon and, with it, a new word that has come to haunt us all: stagflation.

Within the same time frame OPEC, again predicted by virtually no one, entered the scene. It has turned out to be the most successful cartel in the history of mankind, causing the most massive transfer of wealth that has ever taken place: literally hundreds of billions of dollars moved to the Middle East and the other developing oil-rich nations.

And so, the industrial world blundered through the 1970s, not only performing poorly, but also failing to understand what was taking place. When the realities became unmistakably clear, world leaders were shocked into doubt and profound uncertainty.

Looking back, it seems that it would have been logical in the mid-1970s for the leadership of the industrial world to coordinate efforts to return the economies of their countries to a satisfactory level. Unfortunately, nothing like that took place. Each country went off on its own. In the United States, President Gerald Ford made some effort to follow a tough, anti-inflation monetary and fiscal line, but when it became clear that quick results were not forthcoming and political pressure mounted, he shifted to traditional monetary and fiscal stimuli. The U.S. economy responded, although laboriously, and gradually moved up to a stronger growth rate of 4 percent, although inflation and unemployment continued at unacceptable levels. Japan and Europe did not follow. Instead, Germany and Japan, in particular, adhered resolutely to tough monetary and fiscal policies, suffering unemployment and, in the case of Japan, major structural changes. But they succeeded in bringing down inflation.

The United States saved the day, for as its economy moved up, its demand for goods grew and imports climbed. At the same time exports lagged, in part because traditional markets were weak in Europe and Japan. As a result the United States moved into a heavily negative trade balance. In the meantime a new Democratic administration took power in Washington. It, too, applied traditional Keynesian principles, responding to pressures for more employment, with the result that the economy expanded markedly, creating 6 million jobs in 1978 and 1979—an all-time record. However, inflation mounted and the dollar plummeted to unprecedented levels against the major currencies of the world. Here, again, no one had predicted this would happen.

I have asked myself frequently why there was this lack of

understanding and inability to anticipate crucial developments. How could experienced, knowledgeable, and professional leaders in finance, government, business, labor, and academe have missed so badly? How is it possible that no one forecast any of the major economic events of global significance that took place in the 1970s? There is no real answer to that question, but one fact certainly contributes: so far, no country, and very few people, really think and act in global terms. Rather, we work from national information and approaches. We think and plan in national terms, but we live in a world whose economy is global and interdependent. We have not yet built the global model that reflects the reality of interdependence. Instead, we are following national models in our efforts to understand what is taking place internationally and to plan corrective courses of action. Until we truly think, plan, and act globally, we are going to have continuing difficulties in building the level of productivity and economic growth necessary to meet the demands and expectations of a growing world population.

I have dwelt at some length on the phenomenon of how we got from there to here because it has brought us to a point of clear and present peril. The mood of futurists is by and large a gloomy one, and the president of the World Future Society, Ed Cornish, has warned of a strong likelihood that panic may strike as another unpredicted event crumbles what little is left of our confidence. It has happened before in the history of mankind, and this time it could propel the world into a major depression, more serious than the one we now call The Great Depression.

It could happen. It is one scenario of the possible. But another is not only present but, in my opinion, more plausible. So I shall do something that, looking at the dismal record of forecasters in the recent past, can only be described as audacious: I predict that the 1980s, and particularly the second half of the decade, will emerge as a period of universal growth and expansion—the greatest the world has ever seen.

I believe the combination of needs and dangers will compel action and an accommodation to the reality of global economic interdependence. When that happens—and I believe it will, and know it must, if we are to survive on this planet—the enormous potential for growth and expansion that the world holds today will be realized.

There is an old saying that "crisis spells opportunity." The world is clearly in crisis. But there is also a combination of forces and institutions that I think will respond to that crisis, to create not only great business opportunities but also a brighter and better day for mankind. Let me, in the language of futurism, develop my scenario.

First, the industrial world—the OECD countries or, in today's political shorthand, the North—is in crisis. Economic growth lags. There is consumer saturation. A high degree of trade union power and of business concentration erects structural barriers in the struggle to overcome stagflation, while 15 million unemployed, $200 billion in savings, and unused industrial capacity await creative use. However, any application of a sizable stimulus to the economies of the OECD nations risks setting in motion a new cycle of inflation.

Looking just a few years ahead, serious labor shortages threaten the North. This is the product of both demography—during the 1980s there will be an increasing shortage of young people as populations age—and the fact that the highly educated people of the OECD nations are reluctant to do the menial work necessary in an industrial economy. At the same time the cost of raw materials will certainly move up, for the oil most easily pumped, the trees most easily cut, and the ores closest to the surface will have been reached and used. The inevitably rising cost of raw materials will increase inflationary pressures. Finally, the energy crunch and chaos can only grow worse, at least until the 1990s, the minimum time required to develop the alternative energy supplies necessary to support a reasonable growth rate.

There is no need to elaborate further the problems faced by the industrial world. What the scenario shows is grim and unmistakable: the industrial world is in very bad shape.

A similar picture emerges for the developing world—the so-called South. It, too, is in crisis. Population continues mushrooming to an economically and socially unmanageable degree. Massive migrations of people to the metropolitan areas create vast, explosive slums. Unemployment and underemployment are at staggering levels, in many countries exceeding 50 percent.

The demographics of the South are the exact opposite of those of the North. The South has—and will continue to have for the time frame of this scenario—a heavy concentration of population in the age range of 20 years and younger, creating job pressures with dangerous social and political implications. Hunger, malnutrition, and starvation are the lot of almost a billion people on our planet. The demand for goods and services to meet even the simplest, most basic needs is almost inexhaustible. Even in the advanced developing countries, where striking progress has been made in economic growth and, in some cases, in equitable distribution, the energy component of the scenario spells crisis for all but the few fortunate enough to have oil.

But the possession of oil is no panacea. Increasingly the OPEC countries, too, find themselves in an untenable position. Caught up in competition among themselves, both economic and ideological, unable to work out a rational pricing system, they continue to escalate prices at a pace that threatens the entire world economy as they accumulate dollars faster than they can spend them or invest them. Sophisticated leaders in the OPEC countries are beginning to realize the dangers that the course of action they are following holds for them as they endanger the world economy. Yet, they seem unable to get off the price escalator.

What we have, therefore, is a triple crisis: in the industrial world, in the developing world, and in the OPEC world. However, it is a crisis that spells opportunity, for when the parts are put together, it is clear that the problems faced by each are—or at least can be made to be—complementary, and this interaction can launch a new and promising global initiative. To state it in the simplest and most direct terms:

—OPEC countries have money.

—The industrial world has technology and managerial know-how.

—The developing world has the need—and if health, education, skills, and local resources are nurtured, the resulting economic stimulus will generate voracious markets.

This is not a hypothesis. It is a fact drawn from historical experience. The economic breakdown of 1929 was, above all, caused by the sharp, spreading decline of demand among primary producers, including U.S. farmers, that after the boom of the 1920s sent Wall Street its first signal of collapsing confidence. Unfortunately it was met not by a restoration of markets and encouragement of investments, but by a fatal retreat into protectionism. Today the enormous market potential in the developing world makes repetition of that mistake unnecessary and unlikely.

Another historic example of the kind of solution that is possible is that of the situation that faced the Western world immediately following World War II and of the Marshall Plan that was devised to deal with it. To be sure, the challenge the world faces now is infinitely more complex than the one it faced in 1947. Then, in Europe and Japan a skilled, literate work force and an experienced management cadre capable of putting to productive use material and financial resources were available. Further, the plan was conceived and implemented by a single nation, whose leadership recognized, in an unprecedented example of enlightened self-interest, that a revitalized Europe and Japan were in its own best political and economic interests. It will be much more complicated, and require great patience and political skill, to put together a global Marshall Plan, matching and merging needs and opportunities in a new global initiative. Nonetheless, the world is ready to do exactly that.

There is no alternative. The crisis is real. It is increasingly recognized as such. To be sure, North and South and the OPEC countries have, until now, mostly been shouting past each other rather than talking to each other. This they can no longer afford to do. The mutuality of interests is becoming dramatically clear, and the fact that there is no alternative other than matching needs, resources, and strengths in a global initiative is impossible to ignore.

In a number of forums around the world, hard thought is being given by government officials, economists, and political leaders from each of the three segments of the world as to how the experience of the Marshall Plan can be adapted to the global realities of the 1980s. Obviously, much more is needed than a massive transfer of wealth. A global Marshall Plan must be geared to the self-interest of all parties involved. And it must include a working relationship between governments and the private sector, taking advantage of the strength, the ingenuity, the inventiveness of the market economy.

One person who has put some flesh on the bones of the Global Marshall Plan concept envisioned in the Brandt Report is Dr. Ronald Müller. In his recent book released November 1980, *Revitalizing America: Politics for Prosperity*, which deals with both U.S. rebuilding needs and the importance of global cooperation, Dr. Müller describes in some detail how such a Global Marshall Plan might be carried out under the auspices of the World Bank and the Regional Development Banks. The advantage of using these international institutions would be to advance the startup of operations, because systems, methods, and channels of communication and personnel would already be in place. Overall, what might be described as a Global Growth Pool equally funded by OPEC and

OECD countries would provide the capital for bankable projects certified and supervised by the Development Banks. Such a "pool" or "investing center" would set basic policy, including areas to invest and profitability targets that would be used in selecting projects. The investors and the receiving countries in the developing world would each have a representative voice in setting policy and direction as was the case in the original Marshall Plan.

Fortunately we have an institution in place that can play a prominent part in carrying out this new global initiative. I refer to the multinational or transnational company, which has, in fact, been the primary instrument in the internationalization of production, undoubtedly the most significant economic development since World War II.

Direct investment by international companies, based in countries all over the world, including now the advanced developing countries, totals over $300 billion. These companies produce at a level in excess of $1.5 trillion per year, and their growth rate has been close to 10 percent since 1960. These companies will play a key role in the mammoth economic advance I foresee in the last half of the 1980s.

Most of the technology that is desperately needed in the developing world if the global Marshall Plan is to work has been developed by these companies, and is owned and controlled by them. They have developed not only the technology but also the techniques to deliver it. This goes beyond management capacity and marketing know-how. The distinctive aspect of the role international companies can play most effectively—far more effectively than governments—is not so much the transfer of resources as such, but the impact of moving those resources, whether they be capital, technology, or management skills, as a package of productive factors tailored to the needs of a given opportunity or project. This is what distinguishes them from the deployment of experts and technicians through technical assistance programs.

The backstopping service of head office staffs and research facilities, with access to procurement channels and marketing outlets, and the ability to mobilize and deploy all of these capabilities around the world are other important characteristics of the unique contribution made to the world economy by international companies—and only by international companies. These companies make it possible for home-country, host-country, and third-country nationals to learn by doing in the crucible of the competitive marketplace. Today there exist literally tens of thousands of companies, based all over the world, that have made direct investments and developed the skills, the know-how, and the experience to operate efficiently outside their home countries, bringing together the combination of resources that produces the best results.

What I see coming in the 1980s is not a supereconomy spanning the globe, planned and controlled by a group of wise men sitting in some mysterious center of economic activity. Our world is much too complex to be planned. Much more likely will be an accommodation devised among the North, the South, and the OPEC countries that will make available technological, managerial, and financial resources to national or regional plans that have been developed to bankable standards in those areas of the world where the needs, and the consequent opportunities, are literally gigantic. The actual movement of know-how, technology, management, and marketing skills will be carried out by international companies competing in a world market economy.

This process is not new or untried. It has been at work at an accelerating pace since the mid-1950s. There have, of course, been both failures and abuses, but the overall record of international companies, as the originators and developers of the internationalization of production, must be rated an unqualified success. There is further reason for encouragement in the fact that developing countries, which in many cases were suspicious and antagonistic toward international companies, now not only welcome but actively seek such investment—subject, however, to their goals and needs as they perceive them. This very important nascent trend is the face of a new nationalism that enables the developing countries, which have become increasingly sophisticated, to pinpoint quite specifically how international companies can contribute to national economic plans and goals, and that makes it possible for these countries to negotiate a mutually beneficial arrangement with international companies. The same process will come into play as international companies bid for, and execute, the plans and programs that are developed by a global Marshall Plan.

10

The MNC and the Fourth World

This chapter is based on the testimony Mr. Freeman gave in August 1978 to the Brandt Commission (Independent Commission on International Development Issues). It is a further elaboration of the previous chapter, with particular emphasis on the problems of the Fourth World, the poorest developing countries. He recognizes that there are serious obstacles on the side of both multinational corporations and these countries, but he feels they can be overcome.

Foreign direct investment by multinational companies (MNCs) could be a very important factor in furthering desperately needed economic development within Fourth World countries. Unfortunately, today there is no unanimity of support for such investment. Instead, a great many people and organizations around the world are hostile to MNCs, charging that, rather than making a contribution to the well-being of both host and home countries, foreign investment exploits the receiving country and exports jobs from the home country.

I believe this not to be the case, and feel foreign direct investment by MNCs is important for two reasons. First, most of the technology that is desperately needed in the developing world, if necessary growth is to take place, has been developed by, and is owned and controlled by, the private sector. It is proprietary, has been developed at great cost, and is considered a very valuable property by the companies that own it. Second, international companies have a special capacity to deliver technology in the sense not only of technology itself, but also of management capacity and marketing know-how.

The extent of MNC investment in and transfer of technology to Fourth World countries is minimal. Most MNC investment is in industrial countries or in middle-income developing countries, such as Brazil, Nigeria, and Indonesia. Only 15 percent has gone to economies with a per capita income of less than $200 a year, which is where the major problem lies.

There are reasons for this. Today there is great confusion and emotion about, and not a little demagoguery on, the subject of foreign direct investment and multinational companies. Much of the political leadership of Fourth World countries is busy condemning and attacking MNCs as exploiters. In country after country, governments are imposing conditions that are difficult to meet and sharply diminish the attractiveness of the country in question for investment purposes. MNCs become the whipping boys of contending political factions again and again; witness India just a few years ago. The U.N. General Assembly and the Transnational Commission of the Economic and Social Council provide forums for frequent demagogic attacks. MNCs that have invested significant time and effort in the Industry Cooperative Programme, hitherto affiliated with the Food and Agriculture Organization within the United Nations, have been driven out of that organization and attacked by forces opposed to private enterprise, allegedly for trying to infiltrate the United Nations. In many countries commitments made to foreign private investors by government leaders have been breached for political reasons or through ineptness and failure to follow through firmly.

The net result is that many MNCs today are "turned off." There are many places to invest around the world. There is great competition for technology. MNC executives ask why their companies should undergo the risks and the lack of appreciation and cooperation so often forthcoming from making investments in the Fourth World.

Don't misunderstand me. I do not suggest for one moment that international companies are paragons of virtue and selflessness. In the past they have been guilty of abuses and what might be described as exploitation in some of the developing countries, but times have changed. "Exploitation" under modern-day conditions is minimal and is a danger far outweighed by the potential benefits that would flow from major investment by MNCs in Fourth World countries.

Permit me to be a bit more specific by setting forth some of my observations and conclusions on foreign direct investment, based on eight years as a U.S. Cabinet officer with significant involvement in developing countries, and ten years as the chief executive officer of Business International.

There is no doubt in my mind that direct foreign investment is a win-win proposition for both the host and the home countries. The contention that direct foreign investment exports jobs from the home country has been particularly prominent in the United States. A similar charge has been heard in Scandinavia, and to some degree in Germany and Great Britain. But such charges have not been proven, and evidence suggests it is simply not true that overseas investment results in fewer jobs at home.

Preliminary analysis (see Appendix) also indicates that direct foreign investment has contributed significantly to economic progress in the receiving (host) country. This appears to be true even when there have been abuses and insensitivity to the needs of the host country. In that connection it is my observation that the present generation of corporate leadership is aware that mutual interest must be served if a direct foreign investment is to be profitable and secure.

Let me now direct my attention to the realities of the investment decision-making process by MNCs where transfer of technology and capital to Fourth World countries is concerned. There is a real problem of communication between MNCs and leaders of developing countries. U.N. officials, for example, fail to understand that international companies in the private sector make investments based upon a balance of risk and return. Companies are influenced only marginally by the fact that the Fourth World countries present a major threat to the peace and stability of the world in the future, and constitute a great human need and moral challenge.

There is little understanding by Fourth World political leaders that private companies are not eleemosynary institutions, and must be responsive to standards set in the competitive worldwide business environment as reflected in the performance demands of boards of directors and shareholders and the security markets. To be sure, mild statements are made on occasion that, of course, an investment by the private sector must be reasonably profitable. Unfortunately, developing-country leadership too often tends to make harsh demands based on the contention that to make a profit is somehow at least off-color, if not immoral.

There is also a lack of awareness of and sensitivity to the political problems of the government leaders in the Fourth World countries among business executives. Businessmen are sometimes arbitrary and tend to shrug their shoulders, saying, "If it is this complicated and difficult, and if we are received with such suspicion and reservation, we will invest elsewhere."

There is another side to the coin. I personally believe that the decision-making executives of MNCs have a set of limits within which they can make a decision to invest in a Fourth World country if they feel that the political leadership is reliable and that they can depend on commitments made. If there is a reasonable assurance that an appropriate return will be forthcoming, even though in some cases the time span has been extended and the risk is a bit greater than would be the case if investing elsewhere, many chief executive officers will go ahead. This is especially true in cases of developing countries with a long-term potential, which a strong chief executive can point out to the board and shareholders, in effect convincing them to take additional risks in return for long-term future gains.

I am convinced that an effective "honest broker" could perform an important function in bridging the gap between country leadership and company decision makers. To accomplish this would require a person of experience and substance, held in high enough regard to have access to the highest decision makers in developing countries and multinational companies. Such a person could alert the respective parties to a potential mutual opportunity and, if his credibility were of high enough order, get both sides seriously interested. Once that was accomplished, the company and the country would have to communicate with each other and negotiate a mutually beneficial arrangement. However, the starting point would be the evaluation by a highly credible individual that an opportunity exists that may well meet the investment standards of both company and country.

Unfortunately, direct foreign investments that meet minimum standards of return are not numerous in the Fourth World countries, where the need is the greatest. In these countries the necessity for cooperation between the private sector and the government should be recognized. This is not a a unique idea. A few years ago the executive vice-president of a prominent and successful MNC wrote to the U.S. president, stating that the U.S. government and MNCs both have fallen far short of what is needed by way of input and support for Fourth World countries. He suggested a "marriage" of some kind between private and government sectors, and called on the U.S. government to take the lead.

One area in which something clearly could be done is agriculture. I am encouraged that today, in sharp contrast with when I was named U.S. secretary of agriculture by President John F. Kennedy, there is clear awareness that progress in agriculture is the foundation, and the small-farm program the key, to solid economic development and advance in developing countries.

In the developing world today, 80 percent of the people still live on the land. This is where we find the potential purchasing power for industry. This is where we find the great mass of the people. And unless the well-being of these largely poverty-stricken masses of people is improved, there is little real prospect of significant economic growth for anyone.

Despite increases in the production of food and fiber in the developing countries during the 1970s, sparked by what has been called, somewhat loosely, "the green revolution," the core problem in world agriculture has not yet been met: low productivity of small farmers, particularly in countries that have the most massive concentration of population.

These small cultivators could, given the requisite help, transform their misery into relative well-being; in that process they could create a vast new market for industry and services, thus stimulating broad-based economic development; and these two factors, separately and in tandem, would result in a third desirable goal: more social cohesion and political stability for these developing countries. Finally, such action would have a far-reaching, salutary effect on the entire world by increasing absolute production.

It is my conviction that international companies in the agribusiness sector can make a major contribution toward this goal. They can set up efficient, producing core units of appropriate size that will enter into cooperative arrangements with small producers in the vicinity: a kind of contract farming—as we have it, working successfully, in some places in the United States—that would entail the core unit's making available to the small cultivators all the necessary inputs, including credit, technology, and know-how; helping them to clear the soil; aiding them at harvest time; using their labor on occasion; and moving their produce into processing and marketing.

The record is clear that the most successful developing countries in both production and distribution in the non-Communist world are South Korea and Taiwan. Their success, which started with small-farm, rural development programs, built up the resulting rural base to create labor-intensive and finally high-technology industries. Both of these countries have increased productivity markedly, with the most equitable per capita distribution in the world—all adding up to striking success stories. They should be held up to the Fourth World countries as examples, and their methods should be studied carefully.

Other examples of programs that have merit can be seen in an article I wrote for the U.N. publication *Development Forum* (August-September 1977 issue), entitled "Plough Without Prejudice." This article outlines the potential of corporate satellite or nuclear farming involving a large and efficient central production unit in commodities such as bananas, sugar, or rice, with adjacent small producers participating in the work of the central estate but also producing on land they themselves control, getting technical assistance and cooperation in harvesting, processing, and marketing from the corporate center. In this article I recommended a tie-in by governments so that enough land to be self-sufficient can be made available to small farmers once they have attained the necessary level of knowledge and expertise to operate independently. Start-up support would also be provided by the government. In cases where satellite farmers do not constitute a viable economic alternative for the investing company, the government might contract with a company to provide, under appropriately negotiated terms that call for careful monitoring of performance and results, the training needed by the small producers.

There are numerous other cases of success, both in increasing productivity of the overall operation and in training small producers. For example, Japan has been increasingly active in meeting the small-farm challenge in Fourth World countries. Recently 25 Japanese agribusiness industries came together to form an overseas agribusiness development corporation to assist Third World countries in modernizing their agriculture. In Brazil two of the large Japanese trading companies, Mitsui and Marubeni, have moved into areas where land can be made available on very liberal terms to Japanese-Brazilian farmers who are trained and knowledgeable. Production is marketed by the trading company, usually in Japan. The agreement provides for ownership of the land by the Japanese Brazilians on a reasonable and generous time schedule.

Increasingly, large private companies around the world have come to realize that, whether they like it or not, they are quasi-public in nature. We at Business International find that MNCs are becoming more and more responsive to the environment in which they work, seeking to be good corporate citizens by contributing to the improvement of the environment where they do business. By many different kinds of participations, not necessarily directly related to their prime business, MNCs could make a significant contribution to agriculture and rural development in general, and more particularly to the small-farm program in many countries. The fact that over 100 companies supported the Industry Cooperative Programme financially and made key personnel available to keep it in operation for almost 10 years demonstrates, I believe, sincere interest.

As for what multinational companies worldwide might do collectively, I would suggest the possibility that an international agricultural development research institute be created, probably in Washington, D.C., the center of worldwide development programs. Such an institute would be financed and led by MNCs based all over the world. It would undertake down-to-earth, practical research on development matters, focusing especially on what international companies can and should do to improve agriculture and help get subsistence farmers in Fourth World countries into the cash economy.

Properly led and financed, such an institute could quickly command great credibility and benefit the international business community as it demonstrated concern and participation in seeking to solve the development problems of the developing world. It would, if imaginatively managed, provide a rallying point, bringing together international companies to make a major contribution to meeting the critical problem of lagging development and attendant mass human misery in the Fourth World.

11

The LDCs: Victims and Victors of Commodity Price Increases

This chapter explores another favorite theme of Mr. Freeman's: that it is important to see to the development of the less-developed countries because they are the markets of the future. If they could only be tapped, sustained world growth would be possible for both developed and less-developed countries. Mr. Freeman, whose speech to the Chicago World Trade Conference in April 1975 is the basis of this chapter, argues the reasons why more commodity agreements are necessary for achieving this sustained growth goal.

Less-developed countries (LDCs) are no longer victims of world price increases. In some areas they have become victors with the ability to negotiate from a position of strength, and with demands, deeply felt and not always rational, that they are in a position to enforce. What we in industrial nations need are responses that cope adequately and fairly with both aspects of the situation, for their sake and for ours. I believe the need is urgent, and I intend to outline here a number of responses that seem to be both responsible and possible.

The new problem of the LDCs as victors is illustrated most clearly by OPEC, the cartel of the oil-producing countries, which in a period of less than two years succeeded in quintupling the price of oil, and keeping it there. This is in marked contrast with what has happened with other raw materials (copper, aluminum, rubber, soybeans, and cotton, to name just a few) that at times have risen steeply, only to fall back in response to the forces of the market.

The lesson the LDCs have learned from this is painfully obvious. Banding together to further their own interests, whatever the effects on others, brings economic results and political power that they have not been able to win in decades, even centuries, of pleading or reasoning.

This recognition on the part of the LDCs has produced two important new trends in the world's balance of power—one economic, the other political. In the economic sphere, the LDCs that produce commodities the world needs or wants look at OPEC's success and are determined to copy the pattern—with OPEC financing. In the political sphere there is a new, united front, formed by what is now generally called the Third World, confronting the developed countries, directly and in every international forum, not with requests but with demands—demands that are becoming increasingly vehement.

This new political power, with its economic ramifications, found its first, cohesive expression at the United Nations, where it was articulated by the president of Algeria, Houari Boumediene, who called for a new world economic order. It was followed up by another U.N. document tagged, not quite accurately, "The Charter of Economic Rights and Duties of States." This focuses on what the developing nations see as their rights rather than what they hold to be their duties. The document formulates, in fact, what underdeveloped countries should demand of the developed world, both of its public sector and of its private sector. These documents, in a number of versions, have become the credo of the developing world, echoed with varying degrees of intensity but with unmistakable, increasingly unyielding insistence and in a tone that is becoming disturbingly shrill.

In a world more troubled and challenged, and that finds its institutions more critically threatened by disruption and anarchy than at any time since World War II, this widely spread, strongly and emotionally supported demand to reorder economic relations between the peoples of the world is a clear signal. The message beamed at us is that unless we understand the demand and visibly move toward a different kind of economic alignment, the threat of dislocation and disruption for all is deadly serious. It is serious because billions of people are involved, with millions among them emotionally motivated to extremes of action if they can see no sign of change.

There are those who say "So what?" Demands from the less affluent part of the world, or from the less affluent segments of the population even in the most economically advanced countries, are not new. It has always been so. Those who "have not" are envious and make demands on those who "have." People who argue from that corner go on to say that of course we want to have a more equitable world with a fairer sharing of the world's goods, but this takes time and it takes an increase of productivity to create the necessary resources to pass down the line. This argument holds that while our intentions are good and fair, there is really very little in terms of quick or abrupt action that makes any sense. The argument concludes that the world, rather than responding to the crescendo of demands and its dramatic gestures, had best ignore these unreasonable and meaningless noises and go about its business of seeking solid improvement for all over the long term.

Until recently this line of reasoning, based fundamentally on an analysis of the power and ability of the developing world, with its deep, all-around dependence on the more advanced nations, represented reality. To state it simply and bluntly, the basic assumption was that, in the final analysis, there was nothing the developing world could do about converting its demands into pressures to which the advanced nations had to respond.

It is my contention that this is no longer true. Power shifts in recent years have been such that I, for one, am beginning to feel a real, almost desperate urgency. If the developed world fails to respond in reasonable measure to the calls for a new economic order—does not respond in fairly short and highly visible order—major disruptions could occur that, combined with other fundamental dislocations now taking place in the world, could tear to shreds civilization as we know it.

This, then, is the essence and meaning of one side of the coin: the underdeveloped countries as victors. But there is another side, and it is a very valid one still: the LDCs as victims.

The fact is that a period of unprecedented economic growth and achievement in which world output rose from $1 trillion to $3 trillion and even close to $4 trillion—as it has done since the end of World War II—still left a major part of mankind destitute. While it is bad enough that idleness, undernourishment, disease, and hunger are still the lot of more than a quarter of the world's people, it is even worse—and more dangerous—that there has been little improvement, and even retrogression, for the great masses of the less-developed world in this infinitely productive and highly prosperous period.

To illustrate: there are 100 million more illiterate persons in the world today than there were in the mid-1950s. One out of every five human beings in the less-developed world is unemployed or underemployed. Two-thirds of the world's population has increased its per capita income by less than a dollar a year. A billion people are hungry. Abject poverty of this kind is not—cannot be permitted to be—an abstraction. It is a daily pain, a weekly grief, a year-round despair. And a permanent fuse for worldwide explosion.

That a billion people suffer abject poverty on our rich and productive planet is, I hold, morally intolerable and realistically dangerous. It is the great moral and revolutionary issue of the second half of this century, supplanting the issue of colonialism that haunted the first half of the century. And it is, if anything, more imperative and more explosive than colonialism was in its time.

As an issue it stirs not only the developing world. Some of the best young people in the advanced nations, are deeply committed to the cause of an economic order they perceive as more just, more equitable, and more constructive. It is not easy to gainsay some of their arguments and much of their commitment.

With both danger and dedication, menace and morality demanding a new orientation and calling for imaginative and immediate problem solving, there are contributions that can be made by the public sector, on a government-to-government basis, and by the private sector. Many of the LDCs are important producers of raw materials. These countries feel, and with some merit, that raw material producers and tillers of the soil have been treated badly in the course of history. They believe that the benefits of their resources and their labor have gone primarily to the processors and the marketers, leaving them with only small rewards for their effort and the riches of their soil. To them this is the history of colonialism writ large in the pages of their economies as nations and as individuals. Now they are demanding what they see as a reasonable price for their raw materials, feeling that only in this way can they get hold of the capital they need to reshape their economies and improve the well-being of their people.

The industrial world, on the other hand, has in the very recent past faced surging price increases that have proven highly disruptive, and is likely to face another cycle of the same phenomenon if, as we all hope and trust, the industrial world's economies are turned around and head for a new period of growth.

It should, then, be in the interest of all concerned to try to work out an agreement that will ensure producers a fair minimum price for their raw materials and consumers a price that will not escalate to extraordinary and harmful levels. I am proposing, at least in general terms, international commodity arrangements to cover not only petroleum, the most urgent raw material at stake, but also other commodities, including minerals and major agricultural products. I know there are those who will throw up their arms in horror at this intrusion on the market as arbiter, and will consider such arrangements an invasion and distortion of liberal, free-enterprise, profit-motivated economies. I strongly argue that this is not the case; that what we are mounting is, in fact, a rescue operation of our system and our way of life. And I would point out that the principle of laissez-faire as an economic and even a social doctrine has been substantially modified in every industrial economy of the world, and for good reason.

International commodity arrangements could be negotiated that would maximize the play of the market as the most efficient allocator of resources and that could enhance the function of price and profit to give an incentive for production. Such arrangements, by setting ceilings and floors, could at the same time keep price fluctuations within bearable bounds, for producer and consumer alike. These arrangements would be in the evident interest of the industrial world, which needs the raw materials, and the developing world, which needs to sell them. I won't spell out in detail just how this can be done, but it is clearly not beyond the wit of man to devise a system and a set of techniques that can make such arrangements work.

It is true that to date the history of efforts to establish smoothly functioning international commodity agreements has not been a great success. At best they have worked spottily, or for emergency purposes only. But there has never yet been a concentrated effort to make them work, and I maintain that such an attempt might well prove to be workable at this time and also would set a completely new tone in the current global confrontation between the industrial world and the developing world, between statism of some kind and free enterprise.

What I have seen of the developing world and its leaders—and I have seen a great deal of both—leads me to believe that the developing world would be prepared to come aboard the free-enterprise system if it had the assurance that, within that system, it could look forward to a fair piece of the action rather than being overwhelmed in a market that claims to be open and free but is, in fact, quite often restricted and distorted by concentrations of power.

In order for negotiations to proceed toward arrangements that would bring to the producing countries the long-term security of income they need in order to restructure their economies, short- and medium-term action is required from the rich countries, which now include the OPEC countries as well as the industrial world. Such action calls for commitment by the industrial countries to increase their assistance, particularly in transferring technology and know-how to the Third World, and to supply capital to the economically underprivileged nations that are now subsumed under the appellation Fourth World. The needed capital infusion can be shared by the members of OPEC—who have, in fact, been extraordinarily generous already with their surplus income. While this generosity may be propelled in part by political goals—and, as some argue, by the strange situation that secure and lucrative outlets for these mammoth surplus funds are not easy to find—the fact remains that the OPEC countries have channeled close to 10 percent of their zooming oil income into bilateral or multilateral aid.

In addition to efforts by governments—long-term, medium-term, and short-term, offering immediate aid in a number of forms and concentrating on institution building of a basic nature—there is a large role for the private sector, particularly the multinational corporation. The developing countries until now have received only minor or secondary attention from the multinational corporations in investment decisions. This is understandable; frequently the investment climate in these countries has a high environmental risk, the markets are limited, and investment decisions must meet sound return-on-capital criteria. Nevertheless, I would urge that at this time international companies give renewed and careful attention to searching out the opportunities in the developing world that do meet bottom-line criteria. The world is full of bankable projects and, generally speaking, international companies have not really searched them out. It is in the interest of the international companies to track down these bankable projects, because if they want to operate in a relatively free, open, worldwide environment, such an environment must exist in the developing world as well as in the industrial countries. And the only way to make certain this happens is to involve the people of the developing world in the growth of their own economies by giving them a stake in the private sector, through the transfer of technology and managerial know-how that the international company is uniquely suited to carry out.

I would like to share with you something that may sound startling but derives directly from my experience. It is that, despite increasingly demanding rules of the game stipulated by host countries, in spite of occasional outright harassment, and certainly in spite of the vituperative rhetoric attacking multinational companies in public forums, the basic fact is that most developing nations want international companies to operate in their countries. Admittedly the welcome mat they put out is bristly. But most of the political leadership in the Third World and the Fourth World recognizes that it needs help at this stage of development.

The political framework varies from country to country, but there are many ways to work out arrangements satisfactory to both the multinational company and the host country, if the will to do so exists on both sides. Multinational enterprises in manufacturing, in agribusiness, in services, and in finance have demonstrated extraordinary adaptability and resourcefulness. And, with few exceptions, political leaders in the developing world, however vociferous in public fulminations against outside investment and domination, are quite realistic and flexible when capital, technology, and know-how can be made available to meet local needs in a politically defused package.

12

The MNC and Latin America: Friends or Foes?

Mr. Freeman, in this final chapter, points a finger at both companies and governments for their past failures to understand and work with each other. The situation is now changing from one of confrontation, which existed at the time he gave the speech upon which this is based (to the U.S. Chamber of Commerce in May 1971), to one of negotiation. However, the pointers he gives to executives, the "do's and don'ts," are timeless.

Not too long ago Latin America was the first place to which a U.S. company would go when it had conquered a good share of the domestic market and wanted to try its hand at becoming international. Latin America also frequently served as a training ground for young executives who were exposed to adverse conditions and a variety of problems on a sink-or-swim basis, to evaluate their abilities before allowing them to climb the ladder of corporate responsibility at home.

Now, once again, Latin America appears to be shaping up as a testing ground for international companies and executives alike to investigate their ability to adapt to a new international order in which nations and peoples are moving to command their own destinies and control the means of achieving these goals. Economic nationalism is the path more and more of the nations of the

Western Hemisphere have decided to follow, and rightly or wrongly foreign investment is seen by many as an obstacle on the way that must be removed or cut down to a size in which it no longer forms a barrier. In the process many sovereign nations in the hemisphere are directing some of their strongest efforts against a badly needed ally, the multinational company, which can bring the capital, technology, and products the people of Latin America so desperately need for their social and economic well-being.

And what are the international companies—which have contributed much to the progress and development of the hemisphere—doing about it? Mostly, the wrong thing. For the most part they have gone on the defensive, hoping that the whole thing will blow over. Instead of meeting new challenges, they are threatening to abandon the area unless Latin America is willing to play the game by their rules. Instead of a positive approach using their best brains to search for a fair accommodation, many multinational companies are shaping their actions in terms of "what can I save" rather than "what can I earn."

A misunderstanding and distrust of "the other guy's" motives is growing throughout Latin America. Latin Americans charge that foreign investors do not have the interests of the area at heart, that they wish only to make a profit and run, that they do not care about Latin American development, preferring to keep the nations in a state of underdevelopment in which they can easily be exploited. Many multinational companies, in turn, voice the judgment that economic nationalism is just another form of communism, that while nations talk in terms of development priorities, they really are seeking to destroy foreign investment and the free-enterprise system. Just at a time when Latin America and international companies should be cooperating because they need each other, just at the time they should be getting together, they are facing each other across ideological barricades that will be no protection if both parties insist on sticking to their guns.

Galo Plaza, a distinguished statesman, put the current dilemma in a true perspective when, in a speech before the Atlantic Institute exhorting both sides of the argument to smarten up, he said:

> Ideology should not be the deciding factor in collaboration between Latin America and what this Institute has called the Northern Industrialized World. The decision to collaborate should

> be pragmatic, based on reciprocal benefit, on enlightened self-interest on both sides. It should be based on open-mindedness and understanding, not unreasonable prejudice and fear.

Permit me a comment on that statement: True cooperation will not be possible unless multinational companies and Latin American countries free themselves from some basic self-delusions of which they are equally guilty. So far as the international companies are concerned, there is a tendency toward smugness. As one writer said, "Many of them seem to feel that they are clean as the driven snow." Such self-righteousness, stemming as it does from a false premise, makes it difficult to deal effectively with the countries of the Southern Hemisphere.

It is time for multinational companies publicly to acknowledge that in the past they have not always acted properly. There is little to be served by covering up. Latin American countries and the world know that historically the price exacted by international corporations has sometimes been high. Rape of the environment has taken place. Piracy on the consumer has occurred. On occasion, excessive profits have been taken on shoestring investments. Not infrequently, very limited capital and heavy local borrowings have resulted in limited benefits to the community or country in question.

Such abuses, combined with a vivid recollection of the colonial period and gunboat diplomacy, have left a residue of bitterness and antagonism. As a result searching questions are asked throughout Latin America: Will the multinational corporate package benefit the host country in the long run? Is there a danger of overspecialization? Will the business in question become merely a branch plant of a larger operation without any real expansion of its economic base, thereby failing to move toward necessary diversification in the economy? Will the technology applied be capital-intensive or labor-intensive? Will the new enterprise provide many new jobs, or only a handful? What will its effect be throughout the country? Will it spill over and stimulate new production, or will it only create tensions when a handful of new, highly paid jobs attract people to the urban area, exciting expectations that can't be fulfilled? These are legitimate questions. They call for thoughtful, thoroughly prepared, well-documented, and well-publicized answers.

Many multinational companies are now beginning to examine how they are doing business in a particular area, and in the process are studying their own consciences. I recall a conversation with one international executive who, looking at his company's wholly owned operation in Argentina, said:

> Maybe we should not continue with a 100 percent foreign-owned company there. Maybe we should be bringing in local partners to share in the risks, opportunities, and profits of the operation. Perhaps we should not be drawing so heavily on royalties when we are not contributing that much new technology, and should instead take our chances with the plant's straight profits performance.

This type of searching, open-minded evaluation, which reaches beyond the bottom line of the profit-and-loss statement, creates an atmosphere for cooperation. When this happens, a multinational corporation might be said to have become a world corporation. Let me explain what I mean.

By definition a multinational company is one that looks at the entire world as an area of operation, and acts that way. It searches everywhere in the world for new technology, talented people, new processes, raw materials, ideas, and capital. It thinks of the entire world as its market, and it strives to serve customers everywhere. It produces goods or renders services wherever they can be economically produced or rendered to serve one or more markets at a profit. This is the generally accepted definition of a multinational corporation. But I would add some very important elements that describe the philosophy and actions of more and more of the companies investing and doing business across national boundaries.

The first is the internationalization of ownership by spreading capital and shares around the world. Then the internationalization of control, by adding people of different nationalities to boards of directors. Then the selection of managers—from the top down—based on competence, not on nationality. Next is being a good corporate citizen, sensitive to the needs and policies of the countries where the multinational corporation does business. Countries, developed and less developed alike, are concerned with investment levels, reinvestment, movement of capital, distribution of profits, employment, use of local materials, exports, and management control. Finally, and perhaps most important, is giving profitability a new and broader meaning, to include improving human conditions as a central, not just a peripheral, part of business and profit-making targets.

To my knowledge, no multinational corporation meets all five of the criteria I have added to the accepted definition of such a corporation. However, there is a strong movement in many multinationals to apply them. When they are followed, much of the criticism directed toward multinational corporations and, for that matter, toward free enterprise around the world will disappear. Perhaps companies meeting these criteria should be called "world companies," a much more meaningful and beneficent description of their importance in the world economy of the future.

Multinational corporations are not the only institutions that have hesitated to face reality. Latin American governments, too, have been deluding themselves into believing that all their past and present actions have been proper and constructive. Many a government blunder has been committed in the name of development. Throughout the 1950s and 1960s many governments followed a policy of import substitution without a thought to the cost and inefficiencies involved. Latin American governments displayed a penchant for pressing for showcase heavy industries that they did not need, could not pay for, and would only serve to divert funds from more worthy projects. In the name of national pride, governments have reserved certain industries for development by local or state enterprises—only to find that they could not do the job well or at a reasonable cost, with the result that in the long run the local consumer has had to pay the bill in the form of higher prices. Again and again, agreements—oral, written, and sometimes even enacted into law—between international companies and Latin American governments have been broken by the government of the host country, sometimes by the very officials who negotiated and signed the agreement.

There is still far too little cooperation and accommodation by the parties concerned. Neither Latin America nor the international company can afford the luxury of having things its own way without regard for or a willingness to make some concessions to the other. Latin America today is facing an extraordinarily difficult development dilemma. It has the highest population growth rate in the world, with a projected increase of population doubling to 600 million people by the end of the century. In the process capital cities throughout Latin America are growing at 6-7 percent a year, doubling in size every 10 or 12 years. This brings in its train staggering problems of slums, health, crime, and unemployment. Nonetheless, people continue to migrate, apparently in the hope of obtaining the magic opportunity of a job in modern industry.

In any event, the road to development in Latin America is pitted with potholes that must be filled in order to smooth the way out of a worsening condition. There are four major gaps that I feel Latin America must span in order to achieve its development goals.

The most formidable obstacle to development is the area's chronic shortage of capital to create infrastructure and to fuel industrialization. Internal savings levels have lagged behind Latin America's investment needs for years as the area has lived a hand-to-mouth existence. The domestic savings coefficient currently runs around 15 percent, and has shown little evidence of increasing substantially. The increase in gross domestic investment has averaged only about 4 percent per year. The Inter-American Development Bank has estimated that this level of growth would have to be stepped up to 6.5 percent yearly just to maintain an unsatisfactory 2.5 percent per capita income growth. Latin America does not invest nearly enough to get it out of its slow development bind. The area's investment ratio is well below the level of countries that many Latin American governments wish to imitate. For example, Latin Americans are investing only one out of six dollars available to them, compared with one of every three in Japan.

Another major problem that must be tackled is unemployment. Unemployment is a robber not only of a person's spirit but also of his or her productive and consumption capacity. It puts a tremendous burden on Latin American governments to divert funds from new development needs to social needs. According to the U.N. Economic Commission for Latin America, one out of every four of the economically active population is either unemployed or underemployed. Each year Latin America must find jobs for some 3 million new workers and can place barely half of them, let alone reduce standing unemployment figures.

A third area of pressing need is foreign exchange. Latin America's real ability to earn foreign income through its exports dwindles a bit each year. Increasingly its nations have been forced to resort to increased foreign borrowing to cover imports and payments for services, as well as for the retirement of old debts.

The last, and perhaps most important, gap is in technology. If Latin America is ever going to meet its goals, it will have to keep in the mainstream of technological development and not let the rest of the world run so far ahead that the area becomes an economic backwash. Only rapid technological development will give Latin America's products the competitive edge they will need to conquer world markets and to provide goods and services to the maximum number of its people at a reasonable cost.

Where will Latin America get what it needs to solve the capital shortage and unemployment problems, to gain foreign exchange, and to boost technological development? First, of course, its people will have to look to themselves to provide the bulk of the effort, sweat, and sacrifice. But self-help will not be enough. Like it or not, there will be need for a helping hand from foreign sources, which have already committed billions in investment to the area. Latin America will have to face up to the fact that it is not the only place in the world where foreign investors might want to invest. Obviously capital flows to markets where it can make a profit and grow, where it is welcome and reasonably secure.

However, foreign investors would be completely wrong to feel that Latin America's need for them puts them in the driver's seat. There are strong and persuasive voices in the region demanding a "government alone" policy and denouncing foreign investments. Wise policies on both sides are necessary if cooler, more thoughtful heads are to prevail. Foreign investors need Latin America, just as Latin America needs outside investment. The market is too large to ignore. It still provides a good portion of the world's raw material needs, particularly scarce minerals such as tin, copper, and lead, and has a vital strategic significance for the United States.

But beyond the need multinational companies and their home countries will continue to have for Latin America in the material sense, there is a broader argument for such companies to remain in the area. As a whole it is at a stage of development somewhere between the level of the developed nations of North America and Europe and the much less developed countries of Africa and most of Asia. Whatever problems the international corporation is having with Latin America will almost certainly be repeated at some future date in these other less-developed areas. If the multinational corporation cannot work out its current encounter with economic nationalism in Latin America, how can it expect to cope with the same thing when it eventually crops up in Asia and Africa? Latin America may well be the proving ground upon which international companies will have to test their stamina and ability to adapt to the changing order of the world.

Because of the pressing need for development in the area and the determination of governments to answer this need, multinational companies must begin to think in a different frame of reference. The future emphasis of Latin American countries will be on cutting down on whimsical consumer products and concentrating on streamlining production of basic consumer and industrial needs. What's the use, they ask, of marketing a half-dozen brands of toothpaste with XYZ added for no essential purpose to people who probably have not had enough to eat? How can you justify to the host government the development priority of producing 15 models of automobiles when the country has not begun to meet its basic transportation needs?

Multinational companies must be prepared to throw out the rule books they have used at home. There are a number of measures they can take to stem and turn the nationalistic tide that threatens to engulf them in Latin America. My company, Business International, which does research for and provides information and advisory services to multinational companies, has prepared a report on the problem of nationalism in Latin America and possible corporate responses, which I recommend highly to any who are interested. Here are some of the high points of the list of action steps that our research showed to be effective:

—Avoid seeking import protection and tax incentives for investment projects beyond a reasonable initial period, say five years. In light of the area's development needs, investments that cannot stand on their own feet and require a drawn-out fiscal crutch would be unfair.

—Lend help to development planning by the government and the industrial sector in which the firm operates. Some companies have even freed top executives under the "dollar-a-year" type of arrangement that has been made in the United States.

—Avoid being antagonistic or self-righteous toward nationalism; instead, try to understand and respond to its causes and driving forces. A combative approach will only alienate more people than are convinced.

—Prepare a balance sheet of the positive and negative effects of the investment on the host country's balance of payments and overall development. Then develop a thorough and systematic education program, starting with the firm's employees and local stockholders to set the record straight. There is no better way to meet the heat of xenophobia and demagoguery than with the light of truth and fact. Such a balance sheet also provides good internal discipline to keep abuses from creeping into the operation.

—Identify segments of the economy that are ripe for development, to which the firm can make a meaningful contribution consistent with its profit imperatives. Verify the facts with the government and determine if it wants to come in as a partner or wants the firm to take on local equity participation.

—Be identified and involved in attacking social needs—housing, food, pollution control, education. Even if a little money is lost or the operation just breaks even, it will go a long way toward winning acceptance.

—Develop alliances with members of the local business community, who too often view a foreign investor as a crippling competitive threat. Make an effort to improve their business by helping them to manage better as a source for material, or to get into exports, or by some other marketing help.

Permit me, now, to summarize in closing. To many it appears that Latin America is on a collision course with the growing international business community, moving to a confrontation that grows more and more bitter and counterproductive. Clearly it need not be so. The time has come for a frank, realistic appraisal of the total situation. Both sides should acknowledge mistakes of the past, and realistically and directly—as Galo Plaza put it, pragmatically—set a new course for the future, to the benefit of both. It is time for some horse trading, to use the parlance of the Old West. In the long run no deal is a good deal unless both parties benefit. This is the spirit that multinational companies and Latin American countries need to bring to the bargaining table in the days ahead. Little is to be gained from harping on the negatives of hate and demagoguery. Mankind today has incomparably more power at its disposal than ever before. This power, combined with the growing understanding of the environment, can open the door to a new era of well-being for all.

Appendix

This appendix summarizes the results of the eight annual installments of Business International's The Effects of U.S. Corporate Foreign Investment. *The purpose of the study was to test the accuracy of the job-export theory that holds that foreign investment by U.S. multinational corporations causes the export of American jobs by transferring productive capacity overseas that then produces imports that cause American workers to lose their jobs. The results of Business International's analysis have consistently shown that this theory is incorrect, and that actually those companies with the greatest percentage of overseas assets have tended to increase U.S. employment faster than those that are not so heavily involved internationally. The data used go back to 1960 and cover several time frames with yearly updating through 1978. They are based on the confidential information given to Business International by 97 firms, of which five are oil companies.*

A companion study was completed in 1979 on the effects of U.S. foreign investment on Australia, France, and Mexico. It confirms that international corporate investment is favorable to both capital-exporting and capital-importing countries from an economic point of view.

EMPLOYMENT

The companies that responded in each of the eight studies had a better U.S. job performance than all U.S. manufacturers on a net employment basis—that is, after netting out employees added because of acquisitions.

Over the period 1960-70 the sampled companies increased employment in the United States 2.5 times faster than the average U.S. manufacturer; and those with the highest foreign investment increased U.S. jobs over three times faster. Over the period 1960-72 the figures were about the same. In 1960-75 (the Fortune 100 study), companies that had higher foreign investment increased U.S. employment 30.9 percent, while those with lower amounts boosted U.S. employment by only 8.8 percent.

The study covering 1974 and 1975 revealed that the companies that responded lost 7 percent of their work force, but the average for all U.S. manufacturers was a reduction of 9 percent. And the most intense foreign investors lost less than half as many employees as the national average. Over the period 1970-76 total U.S. manufacturing employment fell 5 percent, while the Business International (BI) sample companies had an increase of 1 percent and the companies that invested more intensively overseas increased U.S. employment by more than 2 percent. In 1970-78 all U.S. manufacturers increased employment 3.5 percent, the sample increased net employment 6.4 percent, and the more intensive foreign investors boosted employment 14.8 percent.

The facts clearly reveal that foreign corporate investment does not export jobs. If anything, it increases the number of jobs in the United States. This finding has been reinforced by the dividing of U.S. companies into quartiles of foreign investment intensity. In every study so far the companies with the best U.S. job-creation performance have been those with the most foreign investment as a percentage of total investment.

EXPORTS

In most of the studies, the companies in the BI sample increased U.S. exports a good deal faster than did all U.S. manufacturers, with the notable exception of the year 1975. For example, in 1978 the sample's total exports rose 20 percent, while all U.S. manufactured exports rose 14 percent. Much higher percentages of exports were made up of sales to the U.S. companies' foreign affiliates. This percentage was generally around 40 percent, but was higher than 50 percent in three cases.

IMPORTS

A central thesis of the job-export theory is that U.S. companies invest abroad in order to produce goods for the U.S. market in cheaper-labor locations. This supposition is clearly inaccurate simply on the basis of the fact that the overwhelming proportion of U.S. foreign direct investment is not in cheap-labor countries. But the BI studies have reinforced the invalidity of the thesis by pointing out that imports from affiliates make up a very tiny percentage of a company's U.S. sales.

The first study (1960-70) revealed that imports from foreign affiliates were less than 1 percent of U.S. sales. The second study found that the percentage reached 2.1 percent in 1972, but this figure was inflated by the importation of automobiles from Canada. The highest percentage was reached in 1978, when imports from affiliates reached 3.4 percent.

TRADE BALANCE

The studies consistently reveal that the companies investing overseas have done a great deal to prevent even worse U.S. trade deficits than have occurred since the early 1970s. The second study (1960-72) showed that the sample's trade surplus was $2.2 billion in 1960, while the overall U.S. surplus was $5.6 billion. But in 1970 the overall surplus was down to $3.3 billion, while the sample's surplus rose to $4.2 billion. And during the 1970s the sample continued to record increasing trade surpluses (even though a number of oil companies are included), while the overall U.S. balance deteriorated. For example, in 1976 the sample's surplus was $12.3 billion, while the overall deficit was $5.7 billion. And in 1977 its surplus was $11.4 billion, while the overall deficit reached $26.5 billion.

BALANCE-OF-PAYMENTS EFFECTS

Each study has calculated a financial balance of payments, measuring international flows but excluding the merchandise trade surplus. And each study has found that foreign corporate investment has been increasingly important in shoring up the dollar. Capital outflows each year are dwarfed by remittances of earnings, interest payments, and royalties and fees, and the outflows themselves are balanced to a significant degree by exports of U.S.-made capital equipment and by borrowings abroad (especially during the 1960s).

However one might compute the deficit in the overall U.S. balance-of-payments—clearly it has been very substantial—the performance of international companies is very much in surplus. The various studies indicate financial surpluses of $2 billion in 1972, $9 billion in 1973, $13.4 billion in 1974, $6.7 billion in 1975, $17 billion in 1976, $15 billion in 1977, and $14 billion in 1978. Without these massive inflows the U.S. dollar would have depreciated even more than it did during the 1970s, and the U.S. standard of living would have fallen—compared with countries whose currencies appreciated more than did the U.S. dollar.

INVESTMENT IN THE UNITED STATES

The tenet in the job-export theory that foreign corporate investment reduces investment in the United States is also belied by the facts, although the charge apparently did turn out to be accurate for two individual years, 1976 and 1977. Comparing 1970 with 1960, the net fixed asset expansion of the companies in the BI sample rose 178 percent. Over the same period all U.S. manufacturers boosted plant and equipment investment by 121 percent. Depending on which study and sample are used, the BI sample increased net fixed asset investment in the United States by 60-63 percent over the 1970-75 period, compared with an increase of 50 percent in the plant and equipment expenditures of all U.S. manufacturers. And comparing 1978 with 1970, the BI sample increased net expenditures on fixed assets by 136 percent, while the figure for all U.S. manufacturers was 112 percent.

One of the results of the BI studies of the effects of foreign corporate investment on the United States has been to raise a straightforward question: If foreign investment is so advantageous to the capital-exporting country, then how can it be advantageous to the host country? Doesn't the disproving of charges of the critics in the capital-exporting country prove the charges of the critics of the capital-receiving countries?

INVESTMENT IN HOST COUNTRIES

To address that question, Business International conducted a study on the effects of incoming foreign corporate investment on host countries. This study, which took five years to complete, was published in 1979. It compared the performance of foreign-owned companies with the performance of locally owned companies in Australia, France, and Mexico. The 1957-66 period was studied by comparing national data with data revealed by the official U.S. censuses of foreign direct investment. The 1966-73 period compared the performance of a detailed sample of foreign-owned companies with that of locally owned companies.

—The study revealed that the performance of foreign-owned affiliates in all three countries was, applying just about every relevant test, a great deal better than that of locally owned companies. For example, the foreign-owned companies increased exports faster. During 1957-66 the increases for the foreign-owned firms were 205 percent in Australia, 835 percent in France, and 390 percent in Mexico. These figures compare with increases in total exports from the three countries of 24 percent, 187 percent, and 60 percent. During 1966-73 the comparative figures were 295 percent versus 128 percent in Australia, 297 percent versus 187 percent in France, and 508 percent versus 89 percent in Mexico.

—The study indicates that foreign-owned affiliates increased employment faster, and paid higher wages, than did locally owned companies.

—According to the data, foreign-owned companies spent more of their sales dollar on research and development than did locally owned firms. And they increased such spending faster over the period reviewed.

—The figures show that foreign-owned companies are more conservatively financed than locally owned companies, and that the overwhelming proportion of the expansion of foreign-owned companies is financed from nonlocal sources. For example, in 1966-73 the foreign-owned firms in Australia financed almost 74 percent of their expansion with shareholder (nonlocal) funds and with increased borrowing from foreign financial institutions. The same figure for France was over 68 percent, and for Mexico, over 95 percent. The latter figure is so much higher because foreign-owned companies in Mexico borrowed more than 80 percent of their external financing from abroad.

What this—and a wide range of other financial data revealed in the study—shows is that incoming corporate investment is not a one-shot input, like a portfolio investment. It is a continuous generator of net new inflows of foreign resources for the economy in which it is located. It does not gobble up scarce local savings; rather, it brings in new capital each year.

—The study also demonstrated that foreign-owned companies are more profitable, at least in Australia and France. And they pay far higher amounts of corporate taxes relative to their percentage of the gross national product (and profits) than do local companies.

—The study revealed that foreign-owned companies reinvest higher percentages of after-tax profits than do locally owned firms.

Why and how can all this be true? The main reason is that foreign-owned companies are significantly more productive than locally owned companies, based on sales per employee. In Australia, where data are available only for 1973, they were 29 percent more productive. In France they were 66 percent more productive in 1966 and about 100 percent more productive in 1973. In Mexico they were about 100 percent more productive in both 1966 and 1973.

Index

About the Author

ORVILLE L. FREEMAN is president and chief executive officer of Business International Corporation. He was a three-term governor of Minnesota (1955-61). From 1961 to 1969 he served as secretary of agriculture under Presidents John Kennedy and Lyndon Johnson. He is chairman of the India-U.S. Business Advisory Council; chairman of the Advisory Committee of the Hubert H. Humphrey Public Policy Institute at the University of Minnesota; chairman of the board of Governors of the United Nations Association; and chairman on the U.S. side of the U.S.-Nigerian Agricultural Consultative Committee. He is also on the board of directors of Franklin Mint Corporation, Natomas Company, Worldwatch Institute, and World Future Society.

Mr. Freeman holds an A.B. from the University of Minnesota (magna cum laude and Phi Beta Kappa) and an LL.D. from the University of Minnesota.